GROWTH IN PARTNERSHIP

BOOKS BY LETTY M. RUSSELL
Published by The Westminster Press

Growth in Partnership

The Future of Partnership

The Liberating Word:
A Guide to Nonsexist Interpretation
of the Bible, *ed.*

Human Liberation in a Feminist Perspective—
A Theology

Christian Education in Mission

GROWTH
IN
PARTNERSHIP

by
Letty M. Russell
/ll

THE WESTMINSTER PRESS
Philadelphia

BOOK DESIGN BY DOROTHY ALDEN SMITH

First edition

Published by The Westminster Press®
Philadelphia, Pennsylvania

PRINTED IN THE UNITED STATES OF AMERICA
9 8 7 6 5 4 3 2 1

Library of Congress Cataloging in Publication Data

Russell, Letty M.
  Growth in partnership.

  Includes bibliographical references.
    1. Christian life—1960–   . 2. Freedom (Theology)
I. Title.
BV4501.2.R854   261.8'34   81-7556
ISBN 0-664-24378-9   AACR2

Miriam

CONTENTS

POSTSCRIPT

An introduction is usually written at the end of the book-writing process so that the author can explain what has been said and warn the reader about particular friends and biases that might or might not be showing in the text. In this case, at least, it is accurate to call the "introduction" a "postscript," for it is truly a "P.S." on the text and on what I learned or did not learn in the process of acting, reflecting, and writing.

People often assume that authors write books because they know something and would like to share it. For me it was just the opposite. I have spent three years on a "postscript" of my book *The Future of Partnership* (Westminster Press, 1979). In that book I described partnership as koinonia: "a new focus of relationship in a common history of Jesus Christ that sets persons free for others" (p. 19). In response to the question of how we might still be partners in a world falling a-part, I worked to present God's partnership with us so that we could understand our own partnerships more clearly. But I was left with the next question or postscript. How do we become partner? *How do we educate for partnership?*

After three years of trying to educate for partnership in seminary classroom, church committee, worship, workshop, study group, lecture, and social change organization, I am still left with the question, How do you educate for partnership? And so I have developed this book as a P.S. on the other book, hoping that in the process of reflection on my own action and that of others I might discover some more clues, or at least some of the next questions, related to how we move forward on the freedom journey "with others and for others toward God's future" (*Human Liberation in a Feminist Perspective—A Theology*, p. 25; Westminster Press, 1974).

This is not the first time I have tried to analyze the practice of liberation as an educational event. My first book, *Christian Education in Mission* (Westminster Press, 1967), was a reflection on the way in which a witnessing community can become the matrix for teaching and learning in the context of God's mission of restoring people to their true humanity. Some of the same major motifs echo this earlier attempt at action/reflection on my life and ministry in the East Harlem Protestant Parish. I find that one educates for partnership by a method of participation in that partnership with God, with the world, with self, and with others (Chapter 1). We learn through entering into the process of partnership itself. Secondly, we educate for partnership by being partner; by providing the context of community where people can experience partnership (Chapter 2). Thirdly, this learning takes place best when the purpose of education is to invite people to join in the celebration of God's freedom (Chapter 3). Lastly, the structure of such learning is dialogical as we develop ways of sharing in the art of anticipation of God's promise of new creation (Chapter 4).

Yet such a stress on the learning of partnership through participation needs to be challenged by our present questions and contexts. Two particular challenges to the learning of partnership present themselves to me as a woman teaching in a theological seminary. The first is, "How do you educate members of oppressor groups for partnership?" (Chapter 5). Teaching in a white, male-dominated institution and doing theology in the context of a white, male, middle-class, United States church, I find this question most pressing. For, if it is not possible to develop a "pedagogy for oppressors," then many of us are unfaithful stewards of the talent God has given us. In any case we should be constantly questioning the place in which we have been called by God (I Cor. 7:20).

The second challenge is one that I feel in my own bones, and hear constantly from my struggling sisters and brothers. "How can we learn to be partners with both oppressor and oppressed?" (Chapter 6). Two dangers confront those who journey in this particular land of un-freedom: the danger of sellout and the danger of burnout. People who see that I persist in writing about partnership in a world where some partners are always more equal than others tend to think that I myself have sold out, crying "peace, peace" where there is no peace. Yet I am convinced that liberation includes changing our ways of relating as partners. And I am equally sure that we cannot become partners without liberation from all that prevents us from realizing our God-given potential for life. In any case we cannot anticipate the meaning of liberation and educate for that liberation if we do not dare to image that which we seek. This very vision may be what sustains us when we tend to burn out or grow weary. In a world that is hazardous to the health of all partnerships we have to keep on learning to be partners by developing a spirituality of liberation that concretely anticipates God's intention of partnership for all creation.

GROWTH IN PARTNERSHIP is dedicated to women of courage named Miriam. Miriam and her namesake Mary both celebrated God's partnership in deliverance and invited us all to take part (Ex. 15:21; Luke 1:46-55). The special Miriam in my life was my mother. She was the first to invite me into partnership and to show me the way to walk as a woman of courage.

This book is a reflection on my own opportunities for partnership in learning. My most important teachers have been the women and men who shared in classes on education and partnership at Yale University Divinity School, Boston College, and Andover Newton Theological School. Along with the many other opportunities I have had for sharing in workshops, lectures, and projects, I have gained many insights from communities of learning that I visited across the United States and in Australia and New Zealand. I am especially indebted to the Rev. Shannon Clarkson and the First Congregational Church of West Haven for many examples of shared educational ministry, and to Margaret Maffeo for her partnership in preparing this manuscript, and to Jane Sullivan for assistance in my classes at Yale. The writing of this book was made possible by a semester leave from Yale University and a Theological Scholarship and

Research Grant from the Association of Theological Schools in 1980. Revisions of the manuscript were made possible by many partners in discussion: Madeleine Boucher, Mary Boys, Margaret Farley, Freda Gardner, Emily Gibbes, Thomas Groome, Katherine Sakenfeld, a New York group on Racism, Sexism, and Classism, a class on Education for Partnership at Yale, and the staff of The Westminster Press.

I must confess that I still have many questions about how we educate for partnership, but I do know more than when I began. In the process of writing the book I found out that *we educate for partnership by being partners together in God's liberating action and by growing in our ability to anticipate New Creation, through discovery and building of solidarity in groaning.* To have learned this and to explain what it means in the chapters of this book does not make the learning of partnership an easy matter, but I intend to keep trying to find out more about how God intends us to live as part of New Creation. Meanwhile you are invited to share in this process of exploration as we search for a few clues about how God makes us partners together in Jesus Christ.

1

PARTNERSHIP IN NEW CREATION

Why is it that the longing for freedom does not disappear when hoped-for freedom fails to emerge over the horizon of our lives? Why is it that in the midst of sorrow and anxiety, of groaning and oppression, the ferment of freedom in our hearts does not go away? The answer to this question is related to the impossible possibility of human life before God. A basic ingredient in our humanity is our need for meaning. This ingredient comes to us in many forms, yet at its rock bottom it is in the form of hope. When all seems lost in our lives we "hope against hope," discovering new wellsprings of strength where they were never expected.

The importance of hope in the lives of those struggling for freedom was brought home to me in the late 1960's. One hot summer night I was at a meeting in the Upper Refectory at Union Seminary in New York. The group had gathered to talk about black theology and why it is so full of hope. There was much discussion of the obvious hopelessness of many struggles against racism until a black pastor who was involved in the freedom movement in the South spoke up. He said that the strength of the movement came through the conviction of those who had "seen the other side." Those who, like Martin Luther King, had been to the mountaintop and seen the promised land inspired others to live out their hope.

Most liberation movements draw their strength from such a vision of new creation. Their desire is to be part of a *new order,* not just to make small gains in the *old order.* They desire a new house of freedom where persons can learn to be partners with themselves, with God, with creation, and with their neighbors. It is the balance between the hoped-for new world and the small gains that groups make in the old world that provides strength for the journey. When they are distracted by the small gains and lose sight of the goal, they tend to bog down at one station along the way. What keeps them on a long journey like that of Abraham and Sarah is the conviction that the world of creation is being made new and that they have a part to play in that new creation.

A NEW POINT OF VIEW

Paul describes this stubborn faith in things not seen using the story of God's promise to Abraham:

> In hope he believed against hope, that he should become the father of many nations; as he had been told. (Rom. 4:18; 8:24)[1]

This strong biblical motif reminds us over and over that we do not have to give up hope, because God is hoping for us. In Jesus Christ, God has fulfilled the hopes of all nations by bringing about the decisive act of New Creation. In this act of liberation our hoped-for freedom is accomplished. In the light of this action we see why human hope does not go away. It cannot disappear, because it is hope in a future that has already begun to happen among us!

This is what Paul is saying in his words from II Cor. 5:17:

> When anyone is united to Christ, there is a new world; the old order has gone, and a new order has already begun. (NEB)[2]

In words that echo both the creation story of Genesis 1 and the prophecy of new creation in Isa. 43:18-21, Paul declares that since Christ we are able to see the world in which we live and struggle from a new point of view. In Christ we can already discern the New Creation here in our present reality, and we can live out that future *now* as a partnership of God's righteousness.

Discernment of New Creation

Perhaps it will help us to understand this powerful way of thinking from the other end of history more clearly if we look at the discernment of New Creation that Paul shares with us in

II Corinthians. Paul's letters to the Corinthians reveal a great many problems and possibilities in the life of the church which he founded in Corinth about 51 C.E.[3] His words of advice concern such problems as divisions in the church, marriage, spiritual gifts, worship, and the resurrection. They reflect a pattern of working out his theology in the light of the needs of the congregation—a pattern helpful to us as we struggle with the problems of Christian community in our time and places. Second Corinthians contains pieces of Paul's correspondence with the church in which he asserts his authority as apostle to the Gentiles and founder over against the "super-apostles" who seem to have taken over the church. Paul calls for loyalty to the gospel he had preached in weakness yet with "demonstration of the Spirit" (I Cor. 2:4; II Cor. 12). He also urges a demonstration of that loyalty through a collection for the relief of the saints in Jerusalem (I Cor. 16:1-3; II Cor. 9:1). The struggle reflected here is over the nature of authority and power in the context of the new reality of Christ's resurrection.

In II Cor. 5:16-21, Paul is debating the teachings of the super-apostles and asserting that they reflect the old view of reality, "the human point of view." Scholars are not sure who these apostles were, but a number of their characteristics are reflected in Paul's letters. They seem to have been like many Hellenistic "prophets" whose activities as wandering, charismatic, miracle workers were in some ways similar to the description of the activities of the apostles in Acts.[4] These Jewish Christians used the titles of "apostle," "worker," and "servant of Christ" (II Cor. 11:13-15, 23). They appear to have equated authority with power, making direct and assertive demands on the Corinthian congregation, scoffing at Paul's weakness and boasting of their possession of the Spirit as seen in miracles, visions, eloquent preaching, and impressive appearance (II Cor. 10-12).[5] Paul is able to make such claims, but calls this type of claim to authority "speaking as a fool" (II Cor. 11:21).

In ch. 5:16-17, Paul appeals to a different form of authority, that of the new reality in which the Corinthians live by virtue of their baptism in Christ. We are no longer to regard anyone from *a human point of view,* because Jesus Christ died for all and was raised for all. Everything is to be seen from the perspective of the cross and resurrection. According to the natural and human way of judging things, the super-apostles may seem very powerful, and Jesus may be seen as a criminal crucified in weakness. But now everything is different. All persons and all creation are to be viewed as objects of God's love, for whom Christ died and was raised.[6] Verse 17 declares that all persons who are baptized into Christ are part of a new act of creation, for they die with Christ and are raised with him to a new life. Paul tells the Corinthians that they belong already to a new order of things, to the New Creation in which they are no longer to look for human authority but for the basis of all authority in the actions of God, who has overcome all divisions and reunited us (Isa. 43:18-21; Gal. 6:15).

In his argument Paul hopes that his appeal for unity in Christ will lead the Corinthian church to resist the divisiveness of the super-apostles. The new point of view is not just *any* point of view; rather, it is *a radical shift in perspective,* so that reality is understood differently and life is lived in the new world of faith. According to Robin Scroggs, such a life of faith is the quality of existence in the new creation.

> It is the constant confidence that God has given us our life as sheer gift. It is the courage to remain standing in that place, not to be scared by anxiety, fear, or lack of trust in returning to that old creation based on justification by works.[7]

Paul speaks with great authority of his own call as an apostle to the Gentiles in Gal. 1:11-17 (cf. Acts 9:1-19).[8] And those who have had to appeal to the Gospels against Paul's reservations on the liberation of slaves and women find it a puzzle as to whose construction of reality is true. Perhaps the answer lies in the direction Paul points, not toward either Paul or the super-apostles, but toward the new order intended by God, an order to be understood through the story of God's action in Jesus Christ.

Such a story has to be lived out. It becomes our story as we try to make meaning of our lives and world from that center. The experiences of being a new creation come to us in fragmentary ways along the journey of our lives. Such a fragmentary experience happened to me recently when I lost the sight of one eye in a freak accident. Out of that experience I discovered a different perspective on reality. Small things didn't matter as much to me in the light of major issues of sight and health and partnership with caring people. Yet at the same time my perception of the reality of pain in the world and in my life was heightened so that my vulnerability was increased. Such an experience of becoming, at one and the same time, stronger and yet weaker points to the reality of new life. New Creation is in the eye of the beholder who sees everything in the light of Christ, and in the life of the beholder who is made different by the power of the Holy Spirit.

Partnership of Righteousness

In II Cor. 5:19-21, Paul goes on to explain the nature of life in the new order. This is a life of solidarity, partnership, and reconciliation made possible by God. The super-apostles have declared that Paul is inferior because he was a "volunteer missionary," not asking for a big salary, but working as an ordinary sewer of tents (Acts 18:1-4; I Cor. 9:1-23). (An argument familiar to those of us who are women!) Paul replies that *power is found in weakness.* It is found, not in domination over the Corinthian church and in the use of spiritual gifts to impress the members, but in identity with the One who became sin "so that in him we might become the righteousness of God." In these verses it becomes clear that talk of New Creation as a sort of cheap grace that is easy to receive is far off the mark. The cost is not in financial support for the super-apostles or even for Paul, but in the price that God paid for the undoing of the results of our rebellion against God, and in the mission that gives to those who would share in the solidarity of God's New Creation.

Chapters 10-13 of II Corinthians indicate that reconciliation of differences was no easy matter in the Corinthian situation. Paul seeks reconciliation by refraining from a display of power, not out of cowardice, but because boasting should only be "of the Lord" (10:17). Although Paul does feel pressed to list his credentials, his main claim to power directs the hearers' eyes to the source of power, God acting in Jesus Christ. Of himself he says he wishes to boast only of his own physical weakness which serves to remind him that the grace of God is sufficient for his task (12:7-10). "Here is sick and weak Paul," says Krister Stendahl, "pitted against the healthy, suntanned apostles whom he fights in Corinth."[9]

Paul sees the payment of the *cost of reconciliation in the righteousness of God* (5:20-21). He understands the righteousness or justice of God as God's act of justification in putting things right (Rom. 3:21-26).[10] Those who would live out this new order as "the righteousness of God" are those who join Amos and the other prophets in raising up signs of God's new order: "Let justice roll down like waters, and righteousness like an ever-flowing stream" (Amos 5:24). In our seeing things according to new reality and becoming partners in that new reality, the actions we carry out in the community of Christ are to be actions of justice.

The *good news* is that we *are* reconciled, but this means overcoming our differences by having those who have benefited from their power give it up, and having those who have been weak be empowered. This is not always welcome news, but it is clearly what God's New Creation is about.[11] Paul appeals out of weakness because this is his most powerful weapon, for God is on the side of the weak, those who need God's help (I Cor. 1:26-31). Overcoming the divisions requires a willingness to use whatever power one has for God's righteousness, for putting things right, and overcoming the results of human sin or rebellion against God (II Cor. 5:21).

If we look for examples of what new reconciled community looks like, we must look for an event where justice is lived out. This is one of the reasons that Mary is such a powerful image of new humanity in Luke 1:46-55 when she praises God for the gift of liberation in Jesus Christ. Mary as the first of the faithful represents the church as the sign of new humanity. She proclaims the divine/human agenda of justice and describes what Rosemary Ruether says is the

> conversion that has to go on in history, and between people, to overcome dehumanizing power and suppressed personhood.[12]

In Mary's song God's actions of liberation and reconciliation mean that things are to be put right. In God's "great reversal" the mighty are put down and the lowly are raised up.

It is sometimes as difficult for us to see a woman like Mary as an image of the power of God's righteousness as it is for us to see a man like Paul as an image of God's weakness in the cross of suffering. We often deal with ourselves and others in masculine and feminine stereotypes which assign "weakness" to women. Sometimes these stereotypes have been reinforced by Paul's own writings to the Corinthians. In 1968 I published a *Daily Bible Readings* booklet on Corinthians for the East Harlem Protestant Parish. In the booklet I wanted to change the stereotypes, and so I asked the illustrator to draw a woman preaching as an illustration of I Cor. 14:33b-36, "women should keep silence in the churches."[13] The artist met me at the printer's on the day the booklet was to go to press with a picture of me. I was standing behind the eagle lectern in my church in flowing robes, with arms raised looking as though I was about to "mount up with wings like eagles" (Isa. 40:31). The humorous imagination of my friend Joe Papin had transformed me into an ambassador of God, not just as an eagle who cares for her young but also as a soaring eagle who calls for justice (Deut. 32:11). I was shocked and embarrassed, and included the picture only because I had to meet the deadline and the alternative was a blank page! I was so caught up in female myths of weakness and humility that I didn't see myself as an image of strength. I also did not see that disagreeing with the text of I Cor. 14:34 on the basis of Paul's own statements in I Cor. 11:2-16 and Gal. 3:28 was a way of participating in the righteousness of God by helping to put things right.[14]

Women have a strength that most men in our society do not have: the ability to admit that they are weak and vulnerable. This perception of weakness becomes a double strength as it aids women in relating to others and working with and for them. Ultimately, however, it does not become fully a strength in their lives unless the perception of continued need for growth and cooperation with others leads to a willingness to share in responsibility and self-determination as a way of overcoming unnecessary weakness.[15]

Paul uses his discussion of weakness in this same way, for he admits his physical ailment and need of assistance, and then uses this as an appeal to the Corinthian community for partnership in Christ's ministry. Lastly he himself is willing to become an ambassador for Christ as the righteousness of God, working to establish God's claim to set right all relationships in the New Creation (II Cor. 5:20-21). In New Creation, partnership in Christ's ministry *is a partnership in God's righteousness.*

In looking back at Paul's discussion of II Cor. 5:16-21, we begin to see the many dimensions of partnership in New Creation. In this new point of view New Creation is a dimension of life itself: a new way of living out the reality of God's story in Jesus Christ, and of seeing all of creation in the light of that reality. Partnership in this new order is offered by God, who puts things (including us) right and invites us to join in this difficult way of life as "the righteousness of God."

PARTNERSHIP IN JESUS CHRIST

If the goal of the educational process under investigation is partnership, a clear understanding of that goal is very important. In the discussion of II Cor. 5:16-21 we have already discovered that the goal itself is also part of the process and we have gained some clues about what partnership in Jesus Christ might look like in the present as well as the future reality of New Creation. Before moving on to look at some of the ways that partnership may be experienced as God's gift in our lives, I want to elaborate the meaning of partnership in new creation as it is lived out as a new focus of relationship in the story of Jesus Christ.

New Focus of Relationship

Paul uses the words "in Christ" in II Cor. 5:17 not simply as an indication of membership in the church or of unity with the exalted Christ but also as an indication that Christians are already part of the new order of things. As such they are removed from the sphere of the Old Adam and fallen creation and now live in the sphere of righteousness and life belonging to the New Adam (I Cor. 15:42-50). This is the sphere where the Spirit of Christ makes new relationships possible.[16]

At the center of the New Testament message is the proclamation that in Christ the new history for which the prophets of the Old Testament hoped has already begun. God's redemptive action is viewed as a transformation of life and history that is nothing less than a new act of creation.[17] Human life is new in virtue of a new relationship with God, established in the life, death, and resurrection of Jesus Christ. Such a transformation results in a life of partnership with God.

The biblical language points to a "unity in opposition" between creation and new creation.[18] They are one and the same by virtue of having been accomplished by God's action. Yet the old creation as represented by the fallen world of bondage is one that must be not only restored but also transformed by God. In the various metaphors of the New Testament this transformation is described as present through the action of God, but not yet fully realized. Sometimes the *future* aspect of God's liberation in New Creation is emphasized, especially by those stressing the interim time between the life of Jesus and his coming again. At other times the *present* reality of that New Creation in the life of Christ is emphasized. The New Creation in Christ is already experienced in the possibility of life in Christ, symbolized in baptism, yet it is not yet fulfilled by the complete transformation of life and history.[19]

Such a new relationship is often described in the New Testament as the gift of *koinonia* (partnership, participation, communion, community). The "already/not yet" character of this metaphor cannot be too strongly emphasized, for although in Christ we are already made partner with God, ourselves, and one another, we are still in the process of becoming partners in all the relationships of our lives, and we do not yet experience the full expression of this participation in the New Creation of God. From God's point of view the New Creation has begun, bringing us into a new reality of reconciliation. Thus Paul declares:

> For as many of you as were baptized into Christ have put on Christ. There is neither Jew nor Greek, there is neither slave nor free, there is neither male nor female; for you are all one in Christ Jesus. (Gal. 3:27-28)

In the New Testament, *koinonia* means participation in the total life event of Jesus Christ (life, death, resurrection, and coming again). It is a participation in that life event and in the life-style of identification with others as a member of the Christian community.[20] *Koinonia* is a word used frequently in the New Testament for sharing with someone in something, and it usually stresses a common bond in Jesus Christ that establishes mutual community. The emphasis is on a two-sided relationship of giving or receiving, participation or community. *Koinonia* ("partnership") and the related words *koinonos* ("partner") and *koinoneo* ("to take part") came from the root word *koinos* ("common"). The words appear most frequently in Paul's writings where they have a directly religious content indicating participation of the believer in Christ, in the blessings of Christ, and in the Christian community.[21] Such an emphasis may be seen in Paul's description of the Lord's Supper in I Cor. 10:16-17.

> The cup of blessing which we bless, is it not a *koinonia* in the blood of Christ? The bread which we break, is it not a *koinonia* in the body of Christ? Because there is one bread, we who are many are one body, for we all partake of the one bread.

The richness of the usage of this word can be seen in the many descriptions of the life of the Christian community. There is participation with Christ and the Holy Spirit (Heb. 3:14; 6:4; II Cor. 3:4). And there is participation in the Lord's Table, suffering, and glory (I Cor. 10:14-22; II Cor. 1:7; Heb. 12:8; I Peter 5:1). There is also participation in a heavenly calling, in mission, and in sharing with the poor (Heb. 3:1; Rom. 15:26).

In my book *The Future of Partnership* I developed the understanding of partnership as koinonia by describing it as what happens when there is *a new focus of relationship in the common history of Jesus Christ that sets us free for others.*[22] I understand it as a gift of God in which we are drawn into the "already/not yet" of New Creation by the power of the Holy Spirit. When this happens, a *new relationship* occurs in which we "fall in faith" with God. The relationship is new because we experience it as a new gift in our lives, and because we are made part of the New Creation already begun in Jesus Christ. Together with others we are empowered to share the *common history of Jesus Christ* as the story of God in history and in our lives. This story is one of weakness, suffering, and identification with others so that they may know the liberating power of God's love. Through God's "putting us right" we are set free to live out the story of *freedom for others* (Phil. 2:1-11).

There are many metaphors that seek to point toward the reality of God's intention for unity with humanity and among humanity and all creation, but this one has always seemed to me to be a particularly powerful description of God's liberating presence among us. My use of the word "partnership" for koinonia is like many such selection processes, a result of a concrete event that triggered a wealth of memories. One such memory was that of Christians in every place, gathering around a table to celebrate as partners at the Lord's Banquet.

In 1974 I was asked to give a speech on "Partnership of Women and Men" at a meeting in Louvain of Pro Mundi Vita and the Lutheran World Federation. The question was raised for me, "What is partnership?" Imagine my joy when I discovered that partnership could be understood as koinonia! Not only would it be easier to write my speech by putting in lots of boring footnotes to the words in the New Testament (like those above!), but also I could speak of partnership in a way that made sense of my experience as a partner with others in the service of Christ. And I could talk about partnership as an open-ended process that did not happen only in twos, but also in 12's, 70's, and 5,000's. I could talk about it as a gift of God that happens in our lives, wherever and whenever Christ is present among us as the firstfruits of God's New Creation.

Putting Things Right

God's choice of being partner with us in New Creation includes the invitation and the power to become "the righteousness of God" (II Cor. 5:21). God's righteousness is what we usually understand as justice or justification. It is the way in which God is faithful to the covenant promises of shalom for all creation by putting things right in the world. Paul's statement about the righteousness of God is both descriptive and prescriptive. It is descriptive of reality already among us, that God has put things (including ourselves) right and established shalom. But it is also prescriptive, for the end has not yet come and we are called to struggle for righteousness in the world and in our lives.[23]

What does the world look like when it is put right? According to one important motif in the Bible it looks like *shalom:* all the good gifts God promises to humanity, the fulfillment of God's intention of salvation for creation. This promise of shalom is to be fulfilled in the coming of the Prince of Peace to "establish it . . . with justice and with righteousness" (Isa. 9:6-7). It is described in Ps. 85:8-13 as a gift of salvation to God's people in which

> steadfast love and faithfulness will meet;
>   righteousness and *shalom* will kiss each other.
> Faithfulness will spring up from the ground,
>   and righteousness will look down from the sky.
> Yea, the LORD will give what is good,
>   and our land will yield its increase.[24]

God puts things right through the act of deliverance from bondage and oppression. We respond to that act of liberation by doing what God has done, is doing, and will do—setting people free from whatever prevents them from being partner with one another. God also puts things right by blessing all of creation. We respond to that act of blessing by doing what God has done, is doing, and will do—restoring harmony, wholeness, and goodness in creature and creation. God's faithfulness to the promise of shalom includes both the descriptive and the prescriptive elements of our situation as "justice people" in new creation.[25]

The biblical vision of New Creation sees a solidarity between the whole of the created universe—humanity, nature, and God (Rom. 8:18-25). All are dislocated and separated because of the disobedience of humanity. All need to be set free and to receive the blessing of God. When things are put right, humanity and all the creatures of the earth will be in harmony (Isa. 11:6-9; Hos. 2:18-20). This inclusion of the earth and of all nature in God's action of New Creation is obvious in the biblical imagery, yet this aspect of human disobedience and destruction has received relatively little attention until recent years. The New Creation is just that. It includes the earth as part of that which Christ's death set right, and as part of our new history. Nuclear destruction, technological pollution, and "manhandling of the earth" is a rejection of God's righteousness.[26]

Putting things right involves seeing things right. It involves seeing things in an interconnected web of life redeemed and blessed by God. It also involves recognizing that the term "Creator" is a personal term. For the Creator is one who has shown love not only for human creatures but also for all creatures and for all creation. Just as animals that are cared for become personal members of our family, all creatures are personal members of God's own household, the world (*oikoumene,* Isa. 40:12-17; Jonah 3:9-10). The view of reality that prevailed in patriarchal culture and continues to prevail in our time looks at all reality as a pyramid or hierarchy with nature and animals at the bottom, women and oppressed peoples in the middle, and dominant males at the top. Such a perspective emphasizes the "Father Right" to dominate creation and other human beings so that "Human Right" and "Nature Right" are violated.[27]

The gift of New Creation by a loving Creator should be sufficient for us to see reality in a new way, so that we see all of creation, not as a hierarchy, but as an interdependent partnership of life in which we work to bring to the world signs of wholeness and shalom. Perhaps some signs have already begun to emerge among those who see the interconnection of all forms of God's justice. Thus Elizabeth Dodson Gray writes:

> There is a spark of inner quickening today that warns of significant change—of the turning of the tide. The dominant paradigm or picture in the minds of the world beyond our reach is turning. It is changing. And a whole new frame of mental reference is forming which emphasizes wholeness, connectedness and interdependence, and a different consciousness of self, others, human society and the natural world.[28]

Partnership in Jesus Christ is risky, for it leads in many unexpected directions as we try to live with the One whose own story is about the dangerous righteousness of God. In order to live the story we must know the story. Yet, day by day as it shapes our minds and hearts in meditation, prayer, study, and action, that story presents a stumbling block to those who see themselves as part of New Creation but missing in the language used to describe the story of that creation. "Father Right" is still very much alive in respect to the male-centered language used in our biblical translations, preaching, and liturgies.

One effort being made toward liberating the power of the story to speak for all people is consideration by the Division of Education and Ministry of the National Council of Churches of initiating a project for nonsexist translation of the texts followed each year in the ecumenical lectionary for worship in the churches.[29] As many people ponder this matter, and struggle with the interpretation of the Word of God, perhaps they will be helped to be reminded that *all* are included in New Creation. The mistranslation of II Cor. 5:17 in the RSV still reads, "*he* is a new creation," a very narrow vision of partnership! Once we remove the extra *he,* perhaps, like Isaiah, we will be able to see not just he/she but *all* of creation in New Creation (Isa. 43:14-21).

GOD'S NEW MATH

One thing about God's point of view on reality is that it is different. God's action in Christ is toward a new heaven and a new earth (Rev. 21:1). Over and over in the parables of the Kingdom of God, Jesus points to the surprising reality of God's New Creation. As we have already hinted, one of the surprises is that God has a *new grammar,* a grammar that is specifically inclusive, welcoming all outcasts, misfits, and sinners into the Kingdom and speaking to people in their vernacular, in concrete stories about their own life with God and one another.[30]

God seems to be very bad at math. Things don't add up as the computer printouts from our national church offices do. Talents that are used multiply; people who work only the last hour receive a day's wage; those saved are lost; the many sheep are neglected to search for one; the poor are fed and the rich sent empty away.[31] The good news is that this new math is not a joke! Rather, it is a sign of the new reality of the

Kingdom breaking into our lives. Unexpectedly we are invited to be partners in the new reality, receiving the gift of koinonia as a new focus of relationship in Christ that sets us free for others.

How does this gift of partnership happen in our lives? Where do we look to see glimpses of what God intends for our relationships? We have already looked at the other end to glimpse the New Creation. But we must also look at our own lives, search out hints of how the creativity of God's grace is at work in the midst of our daily struggles. Some of my reflections have led me to describe partnership as *a new focus of relationship in which there is continuing commitment and common struggle in interaction with a wider community context.*[32]

Such relationships happen as a gift; nevertheless we know that *commitment* is more likely to grow where there is responsibility, vulnerability, equality, and trust among those who share diversity of gifts and resources. Because partnerships are living relationships that share the "already/not yet" character of New Creation they are always in process and never finished as they draw us together in *common struggle* and work, involving risk, continuing growth, and hopefulness in moving toward a goal or purpose transcending the group. By definition, partnership involves growing interdependence in relation to God, persons, and creation so they are constantly in interaction with a *wider community* of persons, social structures, values, and beliefs that may provide support, correctives, and negative feedback. There is never complete equality in such a dynamic relationship, but a pattern of equal regard and mutual acceptance among partners is essential.

Since writing *The Future of Partnership* I have continued to test out and revise the clues to partnership that we discover from God's initiation of partnership with us. For they were just that, provisional clues, always leading to revision and change as we live out our stories in Christ. To expect a conclusion would be to live by the *old math* of our human reality. Partnership works the way God's *new math* works, unexpectedly pointing to a provisional and open-ended experience of the other end of history.

Old Math

In II Cor. 5:16-20, Paul has reminded us that we are to see things no longer from a human point of view. This human point of view is a very logical way of looking at things and persons. Success is understood in terms of individual strength and power to dominate others through economic, political, and social control. The "super-apostles" do not sound too bad from an ordinary "super-man" point of view. But there is a *logical falsity* in this view. It finds its strength in logical perception of reality based on false premises.[33] The false premises are that human beings are created to live as individuals who are to look at everything from behind the barrier of their own egos. Such a view from the perspective of fallen creation interprets reality in a form of "win-lose" perspective that is a denial of God's intention for the interdependence of the New Creation. Persons and things are written off as unimportant to the person or group, quite apart from the fact that God has shown love for them all in the Christ event. This perspective uses old math in human relationships, both individual and social, that is *bad math* for partnerships between persons, groups, nations, or species. It is bad for partnership because the math focuses on the multiplication of Number One.

Whether partnerships are among Christians who find their center in Jesus Christ, or among other persons and groupings, they are still in need of perspectives that will strengthen them. Old math thinking produces blocks to the growth of such partnerships, yet it is the world view that prevails in our society today. Some clues to this type of thinking from "a human point of view" have to do with future shock, my thing, circumference, subtraction tables, superiority factor, and permanent inequality.

Future shock is maladjustment with the present because of the longed-for past.[34] It is a particular disease of religious groups and of professional theologians because of their focus on past events and the content of tradition. Those who suffer from future shock become disoriented when change threatens their security. They seek to control their world and their view of the world by ordering it according to a set of static, already established answers. When the world and our relationships change (as they do at a sometimes frightening pace), future shock sets in because there is no flexibility to seek out new questions and new relationships. All human beings need a sense of identity anchored in a still evolving and usable past by which they shape the future. Yet partnerships viewed as an established and changeless order partake more of the old creation than the new. Their rigidity can cause them to be easily broken.

A characteristic view of the world according to old math is to see things and persons as objects to be possessed as *my thing.* Life is measured according to how many things can be accumulated as "my thing," "my wife," "my church," "my car," etc. "What's yours is mine" is the basic philosophy of persons and nations who measure self-worth in terms of things to be possessed and consumed. The possessor becomes the center of relationships, and this makes it difficult to form partnerships that see their goal in relation to a shared task.

In old math, people try to build and care for relationships by marking the *circumference,* or boundary, between their group and others very clearly. Attention to the circumference of the circle of "chosen ones" enables persons to keep others at a distance so that their diversity or different point of view need not cause any disturbance to the internal life of the group. The sad thing is that groups, like church denominations, who "name themselves" over against others tend to build an isolated ghetto and not a community behind the walls. In fact, partnership arises in situations of openness and interdependence. Only in old math does a good fence make a good neighbor, because here the description of neighbor is not the one in need, but the one who stays out and does not cause any bother.

When the world view of persons is basically quantitative and everything is measured according to "how much" or "how little," partnership has difficulty growing. The assumption of such quantitative thinking is that of *subtraction tables,* for when one person wins the others lose. Subtracting care, work, or even food from others does not build relationships. A key ingredient of human interaction is quality and not quantity. Relationships need the qualities of love, faithfulness, and justice, qualities that can grow only as they are given away and shared with others.

The old math of the human point of view is very much tied up with lack of humility, for those who really use this type of math constantly emphasize the *superiority factor* in relationships. They act in ways that maximize their own growth at the expense of others. Such people or groups tend to grade themselves against others to establish their own self-worth. Like the super-apostles in Corinth, they enhance their own authority, power, and prestige by degrading others. Today this is one of the reasons why laity are often second-class partners in the church. It is easier for the church professional to look "super" if the laity are encouraged to be incompetent. Organizing community life by the superiority factor may sometimes be efficient in accomplishing certain tasks, but it is not helpful in establishing the nonjudgmental atmosphere that nurtures trust in relationships.

All the various ways of looking at reality in an old qualitative and hierarchical way help to translate ideas of dominance and subordination into a fixed social structure of *permanent inequality.* Persons are defined as unequal according to the race, sex, class, and other situations of their birth.[35] Such structuring of society may be satisfactory for those who benefit from the old ways of fallen creation, but it undermines most forms of partnership which need a pattern of equal regard in order to grow.

New Math

Human old math is a way of thinking and acting that is part of our human lives insofar as we are in solidarity with the Old Adam. Yet God's new math, as a way of thinking and acting, should also be part of our lives as we learn to live out our solidarity with the New Adam, Jesus Christ (I Cor. 15:49). This new math is an unexpected way of viewing reality in which things don't add up "right." Defying what Paul Ricoeur calls the human "logic of equivalence," the logic of Jesus and of God is one of excess and generosity and superabundance, the logic of grace. As in the Sermon on the Mount, the actions of such math are opposed to our natural tendencies. "Parable, paradoxes, hyperboles, and extreme commandments, all *dis*orient in order to *re*orient us."[36]

Perhaps I am biased toward God's new math because I was always bad at getting the correct answers in math, but I am also biased toward it because it provides clues to the nature of koinonia. As a sign of New Creation, koinonia is more likely to be discovered as God's gift of partnership when we are open to what God will do next. When such relationships are alive and growing, we usually find the gifts of *synergy, serendipity,* and *sharing.* Partners seem to discover an overspill of energy that is greater than the sum of the parts and displays unexpected or serendipitous gifts and the impulses to share that energy with others.[37] Some clues to this revolutionary world view are advent shock, third thing, center, multiplication tables, minus factor, and temporary inequality.

God's choice to be partner with us makes it possible to live in the reality of the New Creation now. God, in freely choosing to be faithful to the promise, makes possible the beginning of our faithfulness in Christ (Rev. 21:5-6). In this way "the future can enter the present ahead of time" as we persist in thinking out of the future even while we act in the present.[38] Such a perspective produces a sense of dislocation associated with *advent shock:* maladjustment with the present because of the longed-for future. When we cease to regard things from a human point of view, then we are also very uneasy about the continued sin and oppression in the world in which we live. Our relationships with others always include a sort of dis-ease about what those relationships could be if we allowed the presence of Christ to shape them.

This attitude of openness to the future makes it possible to consider new forms of partnership as our own perceptions of reality are transformed not only by the Word of God but by the needs and perspectives of others. Once we catch a glimpse of a new possibility of unity we are restless when it remains only a possibility. Thus the discovery of the roots of sexism, racism, and classism in the collective sin of social oppression produces impatient patience for those who work and long for liberation (Rom. 8:22-25). Those who discover how much sexist language does to perpetuate barriers between male and female suffer advent shock in church worship where the good news is preached in an idiom that alienates them from their sense of wholeness as God's partners.

A second perspective of God's new math that is key to the growth and health of partnership is that of looking for the *third thing*. As over against "my thing," third thing thought looks for the common goal, the shared task that becomes a key ingredient for partnerships. One way of expressing this in current terminology is that partnership is to be discovered as "a close encounter with a third thing." God calls us into partnership so that we may serve others. Thus Jesus describes his own ministry in the words of Isaiah 61 as a ministry in which he shares in God's agenda of liberation. God has sent him to

> proclaim release to the captives and recovering of sight to the blind, to set at liberty those who are oppressed and to proclaim the coming of God's New Age. (Luke 4:18-19)

The importance of the third thing, the mutually agreed upon task, comes home over and over again when we try to work together cooperatively in a way that enhances the growth of all the partners. The third thing helps keep persons together, trying again and again, long after they would not want to be involved. I had such an experience lately when I was in a group of women who were planning a project together. It seemed as if that particular group could agree on almost nothing, yet it continued to meet and finally accomplished its task of program design because the women were committed to that task far beyond the limits of their own frustration.

Another perspective of new math that is essential to partnership as koinonia is *the center*. Every partnership of one, two, or three thousand is formed around a center. That center is the basis of commitment and gives strength and identity to the members. Commitment to the center of the relationship allows persons to be vulnerable and open to others without feeling threatened. When this central commitment is lost as the source of strength, then members of the partnership turn to the style of old math and begin to build barriers and divisions for protection. Paul emphasizes over and over for us that unity in Christ is the center of our partnerships as Christians. He speaks of baptism as becoming one in Christ Jesus so that diversity and self-identity are not eliminated, but are focused in a new relationship (Gal. 3:27-28).

In a similar way we read in Matt. 18:20 that Jesus promises to be in the midst of those who gather in his name. His presence in the center of our relationships makes it possible to be open to others, letting down the walls and barriers of our lives. When I worked as Religious Consultant for the National Board of the YWCA, I found that this aspect of partnership was very important in our work as we used our collective power as women for the elimination of racism. Such a task called for the reexamination of the central purpose of the YWCA. As a movement of women and girls it was open to all, not inspite of, but because of its rootage in the story of Jesus Christ. That story gave it a common history with One whose life in God was open to all humanity. It gave it a center that provided strength for a continuing struggle against the oppressive structures of our society.

As we have already seen, God's new math is one of abundance. The relationships of the world are redeemed by One whose grace is much more than the structures of sin and evil (Rom. 5:6-11). In God's sight love is a matter of *multiplication tables* and not of subtraction. Partnership includes the gift of synergy in which even the addition has multiplying effects as the whole becomes greater than the sum of the parts. The overflowing of gifts in partnership is symbolized in the Eucharist where the sharing of bread is part of God's intention that bread be shared with all. Thus we see the signs of the abundance of New Creation as the multiplication of the loaves and fishes in the feeding of the five thousand (Matt. 14:13-21). Gifts offered and used on behalf of others in partnership have a multiplying effect in the partnership and in the lives of those in need of those gifts.

This clue was underlined for me by a discussion of the meaning of partnership at an international consultation of women on sexism in the 1970's sponsored by the World Council of Churches.[39] The report that provoked the most controversy was the one on partnership. Some women asserted, on the basis of Gen. 2:24, that one plus one equals one in marriage. Others asserted, on the basis of modern psychology, that one plus one equals two in marriage because there need to be two strong independent persons in order for a partnership to be formed. In reflecting on this discussion I noticed that they were both wrong. In fact, the new math of partnership is that one plus one equals three or more! There are always at least three because Christ promises to be present. In addition to this the partnership itself always generates additional energy and gifts that link it with others.

An important clue to the way God's math works in partnerships is that of the *minus factor* or calculated inefficiency. God often works in strange ways, allowing weakness to become strength, searching out those who are of no account in the society, and working with patience in the midst of human denials of partnership. Thus we hear Jesus speak of God in the parables as One who welcomes the lost son back in spite of all the expenses of his rebellion, or who sweeps the whole house to find one lost coin (Luke 15:8-32). This is because God's math provides space for people to grow and find themselves as well as to be found.

Such a perspective is important to growth in any partnership. It is more "efficient" to tie a child's shoes in order for the child to get to school on time, but the only way to allow the child to learn to tie the shoes is to practice "calculated inefficiency" and have the child be late for school, if need be. In church congregations there are always persons who have talents that we hardly suspect. To make it possible for them to be full partners in the life of that community, we need to take time to look for those talents. In my work in East Harlem I found that I needed to take time to learn Spanish if I was to be able to share in the gifts of the Hispanic members of the community. I discovered, however, that a better way of carrying out the Spanish ministry was to take the time to encourage Hispanic members of the congregation to discover their own talents of ministry. In this way they could learn to preach and teach and do the social work for their own neighbors.

A final clue to new math is that the gifts of the Spirit are not distributed equally and there is no way of reaching a static form of equality in all aspects of the life of a partnership (I Cor. 12:12-31). What is possible is the practice of *temporary inequality*. This is the sort of image that Paul uses of God's action in Jesus Christ in Phil. 2:1-11. The basis for unity is not equivalence but rather the willingness of Christ to become a servant. In our own relationships there are times when we are temporarily unequal, not by assigned status or role, but by willingness to accept this relationship for the sake of growth of the whole. Such a relationship would be that between teacher and student, parent and child, chairperson and member.[40]

This temporary inequality in which persons change roles and use different talents that are important for different tasks is very important for the growth of partnership. I discovered this in my own marriage many times over. It was not how many times my husband put out the garbage or washed the dishes that was most important to our partnership. What was most important was that we trusted each other to excel, each in our own way, and to be willing to share the responsibilities and leadership as needed. This was symbolized in one trip we took to Asia. When we visited places where he was a guest of Dutch missionary friends, I was Mrs. Hoekendijk and welcomed the chance to share that part of my husband's life. When we visited places where I was consulting with people in the YWCA, he became Mr. Russell and gladly shared in the "flurry of feminist activity." Sometimes we forgot who we were and gave the wrong names, but we surely learned more about the gifts of temporary inequality!

God's new math points to a perspective that is important for all partnerships. They can all benefit from reflection on the clues to the mysterious way that relationships grow. In regard to koinonia, the clues are an indicator of the gifts of the Spirit that God provides so that community in Christ may grow. When we discover these clues in the midst of our lives, we may suspect with joy that partnership with others is becoming a reality in our lives.

These clues about partnership in New Creation point us on our way as we try to discover how to educate for partnership. Our vision of the other end shows us that there is much that we cannot do and much we do not have to do. Partnership is a gift of God's grace and a sign of New Creation, and therefore it is already present quite apart from our educational explorations. Yet partnership is also a response to God's reaching out to us, in which we want to share a new focus of relationship in Jesus Christ with others.

This then leads us to the next question: How do we share with God in evoking the partnership with God, humanity, and creation that God intends for New Creation? If it were not for the *already* quality of koinonia, it would be a hopeless search. But we hope for God because God has hope and love for us. As Hans Hoekendijk has said:

> Christian hope . . . means that we move forward in a world with unlimited possibilities, a world in which we shall not be surprised when something unforeseen happens, but shall, rather, be really surprised at our little faith, which forbids us to expect the unprecedented.[41]

2

COMMUNITY OF LEARNING

Sitting in Butler House Restaurant looking out at
Manhattan's Upper West Side, I found myself confronted by
our next question presented by four women from Maryland.
They had come to have dinner with me so that we could discuss
their struggles toward personal and social liberation. The
particular point of pain for them was the difficulty of
communicating a new form of relationship with their
husbands and families. Perhaps the trip was a small oasis on
their freedom journey, but the best help I could be, then as
now, was to share the question and the pain.

In one way or another this is the question behind many of
the questions people ask about partnership. They want to
know how to teach not only others but also themselves how to
be partners. They want to find out how those already related
to them as husbands, wives, children, pastors, congregations,
employers, employees, co-workers, and friends can become
partners. Stressing partnership as a gift of God is good news
when one has experience of partnership in various relationships in one's life and can name these with joy as a blessing and
gift of God. It is not such good news to those who long for
others who will share with them the mutual trust and
commitment of a partnership centered in Jesus Christ. Such
points of view, along with many others, were represented in a
five-week Lay School of Religion class which I taught recently
on Education for Partnership. Together we were all trying to
find out how to learn to be partners. After five weeks, the best
I could say was that *we learn to be partners by being partners*.
In fact, the only way that I was able to teach partnership was

39

by structuring the group so that we all worked together as partners with one another in the learning process. The lectures, content, and discussion provided the "third thing" around which we could grow in partnership.

This form of education is perhaps best described as *partnering,* for we learn to be partner because others share in partnership with us. From this perspective God's initiative in becoming partner with us in Jesus Christ takes on additional meaning. Not only is God the source of the gifts of partnership but also God's actions provide the model of partnering. In teaching us to become what God intends, God has chosen to join us in Jesus Christ and to make possible a new focus of relationship that sets us free for others. To those who have experienced the gift of partnership there is always more to learn from God's partnering action and from one another. For those who long for partnership, there is the assurance that God is already partner with them, and that in God's unlimited partnership they may catch a glimpse of how they and others might grow together in their own limited ways.

If we learn to be partner by participation in partnership, then we must ask what communities of learning might look like. Where are the communities where people are built up in love? Certainly such communities of learning are not just schools or universities. Nor are they just church congregations, families, charismatic renewal groups, or intentional communities. Nor are they just task forces, mission groups, or shared work or business communities. Just as we participate in many relationships, some of which develop as partnerships, so those who are learning partnership learn it in many different settings and styles of relationships. Ability to become partner develops in any community where the gifts of partnership between people may be found.

Partnership among Christians happens in any of these settings. It is not the setting, but the center of the relationship which makes partnership as koinonia possible, for koinonia happens through the presence of Christ in our midst. Therefore, in this exploration of community of learning it is important to search out communities which name Christ's name and respond to the invitation of God to join Christ in being partners, whether these are communities of two or three, or three thousand. Ephesians 4:1-16 describes how this process of partnering or of equipment of the saints takes place and provides us with a starting point.

EQUIPMENT OF THE SAINTS

Christian communities have always been concerned with how persons grow together in unity with Christ. As Ephesians shows, this concern did not diminish as the first century wore on, but rather increased as the church set out to order its life according to apostolic tradition. In this general letter, probably written by a disciple of Paul, we see part of this process of institutionalization at work. Here are many of Paul's most important themes, woven together with patterns and themes of early Christian worship and teaching.[1] There are allusions to baptismal liturgy used in the areas of Pauline mission; and Ephesians may represent a written address to newly baptized Christians in Asia Minor.[2] The opening part of the letter is in the form of doxology or praise. This is followed in chs. 4-6 by exhortation to maintain the unity and harmony which is the gift of God, accomplished in Christ's death and resurrection. The letter not only describes the equipment of "the saints for the work of ministry, for building up the body of Christ," it also exhorts the churches to be communities where this learning can take place (4:12).

This image of equipment or preparation is one that has continued to inform reflections on Christian nurture in every age. I myself found it very important in the process of naming my pastoral task in East Harlem. In 1962 I wrote an article entitled "Equipping the Little Saints," setting out the way in which Christian communities should join with children in preparing them for their life and ministry as Christians.[3] Since the 1960's, however, I have avoided Ephesians in spite of its powerful images of unity and nurture. Its focus on church unity has often been misused to justify preoccupation with the internal life of the church at the expense of mission and social action. Unity becomes merely uniformity when it is gained by excluding those who advocate controversial social causes such as funds for African liberation movements, support for the

ERA, or ordination of homosexuals. In this regard many who find themselves oppressed, hungry, or excluded have seen Ephesians interpreted to mean unity at the expense of justice and freedom.

In the same way the emphasis in Ephesians on the "new man" and "mature manhood" has been used to reinforce the male-centered image of subordination described in the marriage metaphor of Eph. 5:21-32. For women, "mature manhood" may have more to do with the problem of disunity than with the possibility of Christian growth. It is no wonder that students at Yale were surprised to find this text on my course syllabus. One student wandered around the library the night before class trying to find someone to verify the assignment because he couldn't believe I would pick that passage.[4]

Yet the Word of God speaks through Ephesians in raising questions about the nature of the unity of the church, and about how we become a community of learning which equips the saints. In this context we have to question the assumption that this work of ministry and building up of the body needs to be church-centered and male-centered. For in Ephesians the center is the risen Christ, who has inaugurated God's plan for salvation and unity of the whole world (1:3-10).

The Work of Ministry

The purpose of the equipment of the saints of whatever age is that of preparation for the work of ministry and the building up of the body of Christ.

In 1:1-6 the emphasis is on the *one calling* of Jesus Christ. In contemporary usage, calling or vocation has come to mean many different things, such as work, profession, or religious order.[5] Here it means just one thing. It means that in Christ, God has called us all to become saints of God. The saints are all the baptized followers of Christ. They are ordinary people who are holy, not because of their righteousness or perfection, but because of the gift of forgiveness and new life in Jesus Christ. Their calling is to love the Lord in the one hope of participating in God's New Creation established already in the Lordship of Christ.

Our unity in one calling and one Lord is expressed in the one baptism in which we are incorporated into Christ by sharing his baptism, death, and resurrection. According to the emerging ecumenical consensus on the meaning of baptism, formulated by the Faith and Order Commission of the World Council of Churches, baptism means "new life through Jesus Christ and in union with him and his people."[6] Sharing in Jesus' own baptism to ministry, the saints of God receive the gifts of ministry (Luke 3:21-23; 4:1-19). Consistent with the emphasis on unity, Ephesians mentions Christ as the giver and the gift in 1:7-9. Christ is God's gift in being incarnated among us to show love to all humanity, and is now ascended to heaven, where he continues as the head of the church and the one who continues to grant gifts of ministry.

Ephesians seems to be following I Cor. 12:18, 28 in the description of the gifts, but the emphasis is shifted, so that the gifts come from Christ rather than the Spirit. They are embodied in persons, and they include only gifts used for ministry of the Word.[7] Besides those who are apostles and prophets, the persons who receive Christ's gifts are evangelists or missionaries, teachers and pastors. Marcus Barth, in his commentary on Ephesians, indicates that the last two may refer to the pastor as teacher or what he calls "teaching shepherds," rather than to two separate ministries of teaching and pastoral care.[8] In any case, the gifts are related to the function the author has in mind, namely, that of "speaking the truth in love" so that people are nurtured in the truth of the gospel (Eph. 4:15).

The gifts of ministry are all part of the one calling of God, and help to maintain the "bond of peace" in a setting where there is danger of division between Jews and Gentiles, between those who are converted and those who follow pagan religious teachings, and between all the diverse groups who find themselves members of one community of faith. Peace, blessing, and freedom for new life have been brought about by God's reconciling love, so that those "who once were far off have been brought near in the blood of Christ" (Eph. 2:13-14). Christ is our Shalom! In a situation of diversity the author of Ephesians urges the congregations to maintain the bond of shalom by *forbearing one another in love* (4:2).

The love of which the author speaks here and in vs. 15 and

16 is very concrete. It consists of caring for the neighbor who is often burdensome, by sharing the load of that neighbor. This admonition to love of neighbor is a key ethical guideline for all of the Pauline letters where stress is on building up the neighbor through willingness to live by love rather than one's own rights and integrity. An example of this was seen in Paul's own behavior with the Corinthians as discussed in Chapter 1. The love of which Paul speaks in I Corinthians 13 is directly related to bearing one another. It is more important than any of the spiritual gifts, because it extends far beyond any action of ministry to a relationship of mutual caring. This love, or agape, is a response of self-giving love to God and others because of God's free gift of love to us. Love is a constant concern for the church and for one's brothers and sisters. Through love the church is built up as one community of Christ by asking, not what is allowed in any particular situation, but what it is that builds up the church.[9] Love is understood as a basis for unity in bearing one another in spite of diversity of convictions or need.[10]

The work of ministry means, first of all, serving those who are part of the community. This again raises the question of the price of unity. For if, as seems to be implied, love of neighbor is love for one another, this might mean that others are cut off by this focus on partnership within the community. This is in fact what often happens in the life of the church. A dramatic illustration of this everyday fact is told by a woman from South India, Christy John, to explain why she is so concerned to study liberation theology in relation to the South Indian context.[11] One day she went with some others to a rural part of India where there was a drought. The church had been closed because there was no one available to serve it, but the group wanted to open it and have prayer services on behalf of the starving and suffering people. The villagers, however, refused to let them open the church, saying, "You are always praying and singing and celebrating together, while we are out here suffering." Christy saw that the church had to be about caring for the needs of the whole village if it was to witness to God's love of all people.

Yet the wider context of love for one another is stressed in Ephesians because the exhortations to Christian living in chs.

4 and following are in the setting of praise to God who has acted in Jesus Christ to be free and unite the whole of the created universe (Eph. 4:6; 1:9-10). The bond of peace includes actions of liberation, because God has included all persons in the New Creation. Thus in Matthew 25 we hear the words of Jesus in urging us all to love those who are the least of our sisters and brothers, because in so doing we share not just in our community of faith but in the community of humanity for whom Christ died and with whom he identifies. The price of unity has been paid by Christ, but it is shared by the saints who are called to love their burdensome neighbor both within and outside the church.

Building Up the Body

Christ provides gifts to the church so that it can carry out its ministry of building up the body. In this way the upbuilding in love leads to maturity in Christ for all persons who share in Christ's ministry to the whole inhabited world. The word "upbuilding" (*oikodome*) is a key motif in Eph. 4:1-16 and in the Pauline letters, where love is understood as that which builds up or edifies (I Cor. 8:1). In the RSV, this same Greek word is translated "building up" in vs. 12 and 16, and "edify" in v. 29. The motif of edification or upbuilding is key for the understanding of how we educate for partnership by partnering as well. It is possible to speak of *oikodome* as partnering, for it is the way we build up one another as participants in Christ's koinonia. The word is derived from the Greek word for house (*oikos*) and is related to the word for household management or steward-ship (*oikonomia*). God's stewardship is God's plan of salvation for the whole inhabited world (*oikoumene;* Eph. 1:10). *Oikodome* in the household of faith seeks to build up the members of the household so that they may be part of God's householding of New Creation.[12]

The word, which can literally mean the building of a house, goes back to the image of God building up the people of Israel and building up the Temple and Jerusalem (Jer. 1:10). In early Judaism it was also associated with studying or edification. In the New Testament this word is used to speak of the nurture of the church and of the body of Christ as a community of faith as well as a community of the New Creation (Matt. 16:18; Mark 14:58).[13] Paul speaks of building up as the task of the apostles (II Cor. 10:8; 13:10; 12:19); as the work of the Spirit of God in the congregation (I Thess. 5:11), and, in a general sense, as the opposite of tearing down (Gal. 2:18). The word can refer to the church community in its daily ethical decisions and worship life as well as to the way in which the Spirit builds up the church as a sign of the New Creation.

The metaphor *body of Christ* is closely associated with building up and with the church as the household of God, the temple of the Lord, and the commonwealth of Israel (Eph. 1:22; 5:23; 2:19, 12, 21). It is an organic metaphor for the one church linked together in all its members as the risen and glorified body of Christ. Those who are Christ's body bear his image as the "one new man" (I Cor. 15:42-50; Eph. 2:15; 4:12-13).[14] The building up of the body leads to growth in *maturity* as we take on the image and life-style of Christ. Although Jesus Christ is the image of the new human being and not just the new male, the text in Eph. 4:13 speaks of an "adult man," in contrast to a woman or child, as a means of emphasizing the process of growth and transformation. In a male-centered culture where women were viewed as children, it is not surprising that the word for mature person was male.

In the 1960's when I used this text about "a perfect man" (KJV), I set out to make it clear that such a man would simply be one of the "saints." I used an illustration of an ordinary saint, the Puerto Rican janitor of our church who was a role model for the young people (II Cor. 2:14-16).[15] I was seeking to compensate for the racism and classism in our usual interpretations of the meaning of "perfect man." In fact, I should have used a woman in the picture! Then it might have been clear that what is said here is not about males, but about growing in maturity as imaged by Jesus Christ. For the key image goes beyond the idea simply of growth and implies that women and men alike are being built up by the Spirit to become part of Christ, who is the *new human,* the first representative of the *New Age.*[16]

Building up in love leads to participation or koinonia in the body of Christ, a participation in the New Human being who is the risen Lord, transcending both male and female. It invites us to do away with all the social and personal structures that separate us from one another. As we learn to share with each other as partners, our diversity is not lost, but enhanced by a multiplication of the gifts needed for ministry. One woman I know discovered this in learning to lead worship for the primary children at church school. She thought it was important for the children to have the worship service together, so she asked the pastor to lead the service. Soon she gained enough confidence to lead the service if the pastor planned it with her. Gradually she learned to design the service herself and to lead it, so that the pastor simply became a welcome guest when visiting the worship service.[17] Edification sounds abstract in Ephesians, but, like love, it never is. It is a very concrete building up of neighbor so that together as partners we may be set free for Christ's service.

A well-known image of unity or partnership from Ephesians is that of *breaking down the wall* of hostility between people (2:14-15). Building up the body of Christ creates peace, not by building up new walls, but by uniting us in all our diversity to one center. This is important in education for partnership, because building up should strengthen our commitment to Christ by opening our lives to others. Otherwise the price of unity is a pattern of uniformity that denies partnership by selfish isolation from all those who are different from us.

Each way we look at equipment of the saints we find that its basis is Christ's action in breaking down the walls that we so easily erect in the structures of our church life. The equipment of the saints is the work of Christ in which we all participate as both ministers and educators. The work of Christ's ministry is carried out in love for neighbor, both those who are near and those who are far off. The task of building up or edification is carried out with the One who makes us partners so that we might become signs of New Creation.

BECOMING PARTNERS

The New Testament provides us with a clue to how we might educate for partnership by becoming partners with one another. This clue is that of building up in love. The source of education is the Lord and the Spirit, but the process of edification in love for neighbor goes on among the people who become partners in community and instruments of God's purpose for New Creation. It might seem that this word, "edification" (*oikodome*), is an obscure word to use as a description for education, yet it has many rich possibilities. One such possibility is that it is linked in thought and in its Greek root (*oikos*) to God's New Math. God's Math is described in Ephesians as God's plan, stewardship, or economics (*oikonomia*). Recently, while being introduced at a lecture, I discovered that my biographical introduction had been typed wrong and said that I had studied economics rather than ecumenics! I was embarrassed at the time, because I am so poor at math and money management, but since then I have come to think that it was perhaps correct. For a long time I have been studying economics—that is, God's economics and how we participate in that economic process as stewards and educators.

There are, of course, other reasons for using the image of building up. I was looking for a term that signified the role of the whole church as koinonia; for a word that describes what is happening when Christ is present in a relationship. I wanted to use a word from the New Testament to describe what we are about in educating so that it would be linked to the perspective of New Creation and the gift of koinonia as a sign of that New Creation. There are many images of teaching and learning in the New Testament, for this was an important aspect of church life. As Ian Muirhead says in *Education in the New Testament,* teaching was

> always a central activity of the people of God. The church *taught* as necessarily and as inevitably as [it] worshipped and witnessed.[18]

A word found in Eph. 6:4 would have seemed more familiar to us, that of pedagogy. Children are to be brought up "in the discipline (*paidea*) and instruction of the Lord." This is the word used to describe the Greek Hellenistic idea of education of the individual child to maturity as a citizen of the world. In the New Testament it is frequently used to refer to discipline and punishment as a means of leading. A pedagogue was a slave who escorted children to school and made sure they behaved (Gal. 3:24). Another word for teaching, *didache,* is not broad enough to include the entire educational task because it is associated with ethical instruction in the disciplines of the Christian life (II Tim. 3:16).

In contemporary educational discussion some people use the word *andragogy* instead of pedagogy to indicate that the leading forth is for adults and not children.[19] But andragogy tends to be used exclusively of adults and still is not inclusive of the entire community of every age. It also excludes because the root word for adult here means male as the image of adulthood. The word would have to be changed to *anthropogogy* in order to mean leading forth of all human beings if it were to be used for an inclusive process of education. We already have this more inclusive word in "building up." Here growth toward maturity in faith is understood as a cooperative process described by Paul as synergetic, "we work with you for your joy" (II Cor. 1:24).

Growth Toward Maturity

One interpretation of Eph. 4:12 is that the purpose of equipping the saints is so that they can carry out the work of ministry and upbuilding of the body. If we ask *how* to equip the saints, we find that the purpose is also the method. People grow toward maturity in Christ by participating in the work of service and mutual partnering. They grow toward the Center, Jesus Christ, by sharing in the "third thing" of his own life: ministry or service of neighbor. The gifts that make it possible to *grow by doing* are the gifts of the Spirit granted to members of the congregation for its upbuilding in service. The gifts are a sign that the New Creation, already begun in Jesus Christ, is already at work among the members of the congregation (Rom. 8:23).

The maturity of which Ephesians speaks is linked to the New Creation. It is not as individuals that we move toward "the fulness of Christ" (Eph. 4:13). It is as members of the body of Christ, already linked to Christ in baptism, that we grow toward the full unity in Christ in the New Creation. Growth toward maturity is *growth toward Christ,* as part of a present community of service and partnership and as part of the future community of shalom in the New Creation. If it is growth toward Christ, then the major clues to this growth are related to the ways in which a new focus of relationship in Christ transforms our lives, and the way that relationship and shared story sets us free for others.

Usually we speak of our response to Christ's call as conversion, a sudden or lengthy process of turning around and reorienting our life so that Christ is at the center. This new focus of relationship is one of faith or trust that God loves us in Jesus Christ. The New Testament understanding of faith has three overlapping and interrelated dimensions. The first is that of *confidence* that God has faith in us and is faithful to us so that nothing can separate us from the love of God in Jesus Christ. The second is *knowledge* of the liberating actions of God in Christ and the story of those actions. The third is *consent* to take part in those actions by trying out what the story of God's love affair with the world means in our own lives.[20] Faith as a gift of God happens in our lives in all three ways as we grow as members of Christ's body. Different aspects of faith receive more or less emphasis at various times in our lives, but they are not sequential stages. They are a continuing spiral of growth, not a ladder sequence. The dimensions of faith are ever-changing ways the Spirit works through our lives in building us together in the body of Christ.

Another way of describing growth in faith is to use the analysis of *faith development* proposed by James Fowler. He speaks of faith as a structured way of knowing which provides a framework of meaning and value, but is not necessarily synonymous with religion or belief.[21] Faith is a knowing or construing by which persons apprehend themselves as related to the transcendent. It is understood both as external world maintenance in a shared vision of reality and as internal knowing and construing in a patterned process. Stage theory focuses on the structure of this internal process of knowing. Fowler's work builds on that of Erikson in psychosocial development, Piaget in cognitive development, and Kohlberg in moral development. Relating his six stages to those of Kohlberg, Fowler nevertheless maintains that faith is the basic orientation in the world by which a person maintains human meaning and that moral decision-making is derived from that.[22]

These different ways of organizing our beliefs and values always occur in the same order in any individual, although a person probably will not move through all six stages in a lifetime. Each stage builds on the previous stages and no person skips over a stage. As a result of interviews and testing, Fowler describes six stages, and the minimum age at which it is possible to arrive at that stage.

1. *Intuitive-Projective Faith.* Imitating primal adults, with little distinction between fact and fantasy. Age 4. "Early childhood and the birth of imagination."

2. *Mythic-Literal Faith.* Beliefs and attitudes appropriated with literal interpretations, and appeal to authority. Ages 6½-8. "Childhood and the delight in narrative and drama."

3. *Synthetic-Conventional Faith.* Relating to a variety of worlds beyond the family on the basis of conventional wisdom and authority of those who count. Ages 12-13. "Adolescence with its quest for personal truth and its romance of vision and fidelity."

4. *Individuating-Reflexive Faith.* Attempts at synthesis of world with appeal to alternative faith claims and ideologies, and growth of self-awareness and responsibility for choices. Ages 18-19. "Young adulthood, its thirst for ideology and courage of the single eye."

5. *Paradoxical-Consolidative Faith.* Affirmation of the paradoxical, appreciation of traditions of self and others, espousal of beliefs congruent with risk and action taken. Ages 30-32. "Adulthood and its suffering vicarage for the world."

6. *Universalizing Faith.* A rare stage, with sense of oneness of all persons and a vision of universal inclusiveness. Ages 38-40. "The saintly universal with its costly actualization of the coming kingdom of God."[23]

This very sketchy and oversimplified version of Fowler's stages does not do justice to them, and the elaborate theory and its documentation needs to be studied in current articles as well as in a full-length book he has promised us. The stages themselves are complex and difficult to identify and the titles are not very illuminating. Different people have tried to simplify the titles in various ways. One way, suggested by Sharon Parks of Harvard Divinity School, who studied with Fowler, is to describe the developmental process as a movement through *dependence, counterdependence, selfdependence,* and *interdependence.*[24] John Westerhoff has been helpful in relating the stages to the faith community and in calling them *faith styles* rather than stages, because they are all equally faith and equally valid ways of faith knowing. In his book *Will Our Children Have Faith?* Westerhoff speaks of faith as *experienced* in childhood through interaction with other faithing selves; of faith as *affiliative* through opportunity to participate in a self-conscious community of faith as *searching* through doubt, critical judgment, and experimentation; of faith as *ownership* in putting faith into personal and social action.[25]

Fowler has worked out his theory and compared it with other related theories in great detail. His is a very creative attempt to speak of maturity and its development in descriptive categories that can inform our understanding religious growth. As a theologian, Fowler admits that his stages have a normative end point. His vision of universalizing faith and full maturity is that of the Kingdom of God.[26] It is toward this future of God that the stages of faith proceed. In this sense they are not value free, but rather test out certain hypotheses concerning how people mature. Such studies often find what they are looking for in the interviews. Their data are also influenced by the sex, race, religion, privilege, and culture of those studied even though they claim that the stages are universally valid for all human beings. In the case of Lawrence Kohlberg, on whom Fowler leans for his six stages, the data bias is a real drawback. The original basis of the stages evolved from interviews of 50 Chicago-area males, middle class and working class, ages ten to sixteen. These subjects have been interviewed every three years since 1958.[27] In addition, the stages underline a linear, hierarchical, and cognitive development and do not take into account other ways of developing through interpersonal and negotiated relationships, or social interactional models.[28]

When such a construct is imposed on all persons in the assumption that it is an accurate description of the way they assign meaning to the world, there is danger of injustice. In the name of looking for easy solutions in areas of religious education, bias against those who do not happen to fit the original categories may perpetuate the very problems in development that the research was designed to cure. Fowler himself cautions about jumping to conclusions. He has tried to correct some of the bias in his studies begun in 1972, and thinks of them as tentative models, descriptive and not prescriptive of the faith process.

> Above all we want to avoid the nefarious misuses of this stage theory that would make of it a value scale to determine the relative worth of persons or groups. Each stage may be *the* appropriate stage for a particular person or group. Each stage describes a pattern of valuing, thinking, feeling and committing that is potentially worthy, serene and "graceful."[29]

In using the stages to design curriculum and develop teaching styles that facilitate faith development, we need to take great care not to assume that we can know and evaluate a person's faith.[30] Even though the stages are ways of describing the structured process of assigning meaning to the world, they are not indications of growth of the trusting relationship to God that underlines the Christian understanding of faith. One is related to the other, and there is always the danger of making *judgments of faith*. From the Christian perspective, faith is a gift of God and only God can search our hearts to know the full meaning of that relationship. Often we look at actions, attitudes, and ways of answering questions as ways of judging faith rather than as ways of seeing how a person's life is being shaped as part of God's story of faith.

An important aspect of developmental theory is not the stages themselves but the research on how people move through the crises and passages from one stage to another.[31] For growth toward maturity means something more than socialization or shaping of persons by their society and culture into the status quo. Critical awareness can be promoted by facilitating the crises that lead persons and groups to think in new, more critical ways. In this regard, developmental theory may provide clues to how our horizons can expand until we are able to respond more fully as partners to one another.

Kohlberg is helpful here in describing how one moves from one stage to another in moral development toward a fuller understanding of justice as a primary regard for the value and equality of all human beings and for reciprocity in human relations.[32]

Change to a new stage can be promoted through participation in a variety of social experiences with opportunity to take different roles and encounter other perspectives. Such exposure leads to *cognitive conflict* in which one's pattern of decision-making and view of the world no longer seem adequate for experience. This conflict can be increased to assist the person to move toward a new stage by what Kohlberg calls *exposure to the next stage* of reasoning above one's own. Persons prefer and assimilate reasoning at the highest stage they understand and they are often able to understand the reasoning of the next higher stage. They understand the stages below them but reject them as a way of reasoning. At such moments three elements are very important for growth. One is a social context representing cultural, racial, and economic diversity. Another is a supportive community of persons that makes it easier to risk new decisions amd actions. The other is a significant person who provides the stimulation of thinking at a "higher" stage. The teaching ministry of the church in many ways can provide possibility for that diversity, support, and exposure to more developed expressions of faith.

Partnership Development

Fowler speaks of faith as a verb or an activity and has used the word "faithing" as a description of the process of development. Such a word would help to make the distinction between *faithing* as a way of knowing and construing the world and a *faith* as it is understood in the New Testament as a gift of God. Our faith relationship of trust in God is a response to God's faith in us. The response includes confidence in God's love, knowledge of the story of that love in Jesus Christ, and consent to live out that story in love for our neighbor. This relationship of faith underlies any and all the stages, and at any one stage all of these dimensions of faith might be present. For instance, the adolescent might be in a synthetic-conventional stage and be more interested in testing faith through consent to try it out, yet both knowledge and confidence would have to be present in order to be tested. Our view of reality, our way of faithing and knowing, is already shaped by the One who is the truth, "the Amen," the one who is *faithful* in reaching out to make us partners in the work of New Creation. Through the words of the Spirit we experience in our lives,

> the words of the Amen, the faithful and true witness, the beginning of God's creation. (Rev. 3:14)

Even when we distinguish between the process of faithing and faith we still find that faith development is not what is being hinted at in the description in Ephesians of upbuilding the Christian community. For in Ephesians maturity is not thought of as some individual quest, but as the development of the whole church as a partnership in the body of Christ which is an anticipation of God's intended future. Insofar as one would talk about ways of knowing the world through faith, this would represent a collective process of building up in love in which each person ministers to the other, bringing gifts of the Spirit. Together Christian communities would move from dependence to counterdependence, to selfdependence, and, finally, toward interdependence.

The perspective of edification of the body leads us to investigate the context of growth in the whole church that invites persons to become partners in the sharing of community. This underlines the organic nature of growth which takes place as social interaction between persons.[33] *Styles of partnership development* would then focus on the ways in which congregations develop as nurturing and partnering communities where persons can experience faith as shaping life. Such an attempt to find stages of partnership development would need extensive field testing and social analysis, beginning with self-study of congregations. But for the purpose of underlining the need for growth in partnership we could discuss various styles that would not be an invariable sequence of stages. As a typology of *church styles* they all present ways of developing toward partnership and they all would have within their membership persons of all stages of faithing.

The two clues about partnership that have emerged as themes in our study of building up are those of "centering in Christ" and "the common agenda, task or third thing."[34] Using these as indicators of style, I will try to suggest a typology of partnership development, following the ideas of Fowler and the titles suggested by Sharon Parks.[35] It will begin from the other end, recognizing that none of these styles are fully part of New Creation (Stage 6?), but that all of them represent signs of growth into maturity in Christ and thus into New Creation.

Building up toward partnership would seek to develop a style of church life as *interdependence*. Here the dialectic between critically chosen beliefs and norms and those of other groups and traditions is recognized. The commitment to Christ at the center becomes a foundation for risk and action. Boundaries are more open as the needs of God's world are seen as the third thing of the church's mission. The style of *selfdependence* would be seen in a church community that seeks to make its own faith claims clear over against those of other faiths and ideologies. Its relation to the center is clarified by means of attention to boundaries, and the commitment to a third thing tends to be that of actions that clarify distinction from other groups. The style of *counterdependence* recognizes authority as invested in certain individuals and teachings that represent Christ the center. Its major common agenda is that of testing out the perceived center by searching for its own alternative style of truth. *Dependence* is a style of church life in which persons accept authority as representative of Christ and identify their common commitment to action as the maintenance of that authority.

This is a dangerous typology, because it too might be used for evaluation rather than as a means of understanding how congregations grow as communities where partnership happens. Church communities are never really of only one style and they can all move from where they are toward the style of interdependence. Insofar as they represent different theological styles we could say that churches of selfdependent style would be attracted to liberation theologies. Churches of counterdependent style would be more apt to opt for liberal theological positions and those which are dependent would be more likely to have conservative views of biblical or church authority.

To take one further example, we can ask how each style would lead to the use or rejection of the common ecumenical lectionary for worship and preaching among Protestant and Roman Catholic churches.[36] Interdependent styles would see a common lectionary as an opportunity for nurture of the entire congregation through study as well as worship and as a way of living out unity in diversity. Selfdependent and counterdependent styles might lead toward ways of selecting texts more helpful to identity development, while dependent styles would find the lectionary an important source of certainty and a link to historical tradition.

When a congregation stays in one style for too long, with no crisis and growth, it will lose its ability to grow and change, and will become rigid. Perhaps, then, the most important part of the styles of partnership is not which style, but whether there is continuing organic growth that encourages members in becoming partners.

EDUCATIONAL MINISTRY

Grace has been given to each of us according to the measure of Christ's gift.

And his gifts were that some should be apostles, some prophets, some evangelists, some pastors and teachers, to equip the saints. (Eph. 4:11-12)

The community of learning is Spirit-filled and it is by the power of the Spirit of Christ that the ministry takes place. The ministry is one because it is Christ's ministry, but the exercise of gifts in ministry is diverse. The ministry is a service of the gospel in proclamation of its message that in Christ the walls of sin and oppression that divide us from ourselves, others, and God have been broken down (Eph. 2:13-18). It is also an educational ministry that draws the whole community into God's service and invites others to come along as partners in the journey toward God's future. The persons who have received gifts to enable the community in its educational ministry are called teaching pastors in Ephesians 4.

Teaching Pastors

Although the RSV translates v. 11 as "pastors and teachers," the two words belong closer together than apostles, prophets, and evangelists in the Greek wording, where they stand as a pair.[37] The pastoral or shepherd role was understood to include that of teaching in the New Testament, but it is teaching that is prominent in Paul's more extensive lists of gifts in I Cor. 12:28-29 and Rom. 12:6-8. There were many gifts of ministry recognized in the early church and they were combined in various ways. Here it appears that the teaching pastor is considered important to the church's work of ministry and to building up into unity in Christ. In spite of diverse gifts and roles, the one ministry of the whole church to and for the world is not to be divided. Pastoral care is not separate from teaching, nor from apostolic witness, prophecy, or evangelistic service. There is no need to think that education for partnership is a task separate from the worshiping and serving life of the congregation.

One way of seeking to recapture this sense of unity in ministry is to think of the task of building up the body as the congregation's task of educational ministry. *Educational ministry* refers to any form of serving in the name of Jesus Christ that involves us in mutual growth and fuller self-actualization of God's intended humanity.[38] Its goal is the development of critical and committed awareness among persons as they serve in Christ's name and seek to be a sign of God's New Creation. In Christian communities the presence of the One who came "not to be served but to serve" empowers all members of the community for service and not just the women or the clergy (Matt. 20:28). As Rosemary Ruether puts it:

> The principles of Christian community are founded upon a role transformation between men and women, rulers and ruled. The ministry of the Church is not to be modeled on hierarchies of lordship, but on the *diakonia* of women and servants, while women are freed from exclusive identification with the service role and called to join the circle of disciples as equal members.[39]

Such service or ministry in the beginning of the New Creation is possible because all persons find their primary identity, not in their assigned sex, race, or class, but in Jesus Christ, who sets them free for service.

Educational ministry includes *diakonia,* as the acceptance of someone else's life project as our own scenario or story. It begins with accepting Jesus' own story as our own and then extends to solidarity with others. Acts 6:1-6 indicates that the early church saw this role of caring for the widows and the poor as a task without much glamour. Hans Hoekendijk describes it as "functioning as a waiter, that is to be subordinate, to be inconspicuous, to be available, ready to give a hand."[40] It also includes *education* understood as a process of actualizing and modifying the development of the total person in and through dialogical relationships.[41] Ministry is educational when it offers the possibility of growth in ability to serve others. In one sense all ministry is educational whether or not this is intended, for human beings learn from their social environment through the enculturation process. We learn through participation in a faith community which communicates the meaning of ministry which is practiced in that community. In another sense ministry can be intentionally educational when there is a process of partnership in learning so that persons of all ages are invited to join in God's continuing actions. Describing the teaching pastoral role of the church as educational ministry has the possibility of beginning beyond the dichotomies of ministry/education; clergy/educators; teachers/students; clergy/congregation; church/world. As Christians we all share in Christ's ministry or service and thus we are all involved in a lifelong process of becoming partners.

This more holistic perspective on the educational ministry of the congregation might also provide an opportunity for an alternative model for "professional ministry" in the church.[42] This ministry of educators has long had an image of inferiority in church and society. Women, children, and religious education seem to go together. The educators are usually the "misfits" in the power structure who work "behind the scenes." Frequently they are separated from the liturgical life of the church and from continuing theological education.[43] Yet educational ministry is an important *alternative style of ministry* for both men and women who are searching for a role model of *enabler.* It is a style of ministry that is open to ordained and unordained alike, and one that can encourage partnership with others both inside and outside the church.

This alternative needs to be developed so that the educational task is claimed as a full and equal style of service in which liturgy, action, and nurture all represent aspects of church life that can be intentionally and cooperatively educational. Already existing educational associations and networks may be able to provide the basis of developing groups of women and men who are committed to "subverting the church" into being a church of mutual upbuilding, and to using their "misfit" position as a means of freedom in ministry and advocacy for others who are considered "misfits." As we shall see in Chapter 4, theological resources in the area of liberation theologies are being developed that provide opportunities for doing theology in partnership.

In testing out whether a congregation and its chosen enablers are working toward partnership in educational ministry we can ask questions about congregational life in the light of three clues from God's New Math. The first clue is that of *temporary inequality.* Is there opportunity for teachers to be taught by their students and one another? Is there a shifting around of roles and a sharing of leadership so that all persons grow in the work of ministry shared in Sunday worship?[44] Educational ministry is growing when a wide variety of persons of all ages, sexes, and racial groups participate in conducting the educational program and the worship service and enjoy this teamwork.

The second clue important to educational ministry is the *minus factor.* How many things does the pastor or educator not do so that there is space in the program for others to develop their gifts? One pastor I know was so effective at getting others to share in the programs of the vacation church school that a child attending the school went up to the pastor and said, "What do you do here?"

The third clue is *multiplication tables.* Is the educational ministry a self-building up of the congregation so that it constantly involves more people and more gifts in service? One teacher recognized this need by focusing on the improvement of the entire group of emotionally disturbed children in her class. All the activities were designed to let the group learn to use their gifts of self-control, decision-making, and mutual teaching so that opportunities for learning multiplied through the interaction of the group.[45]

Those who practice educational ministry do not have to fear loss of leadership in the church, because, in fact, the key to good leadership is service. One can learn how to lead when this is needed for servant/leadership, but the first gift needed by all in the work of ministry is the ability to serve.[46]

Breaking Down the Walls

Christ has broken down the dividing walls between members in the church, between clergy and laity, and between the church and the world. The ministry and the gifts of ministry are already a sign of God's New Creation in which all will be united together in partnership with God. Ministry understood from this perspective should contribute to unity rather than representing divisions of class, authority, and power. At the other end of history there are to be no divisions between clergy and people or church and world. This, for instance, is the image of New Jerusalem in Revelation, where there is no longer any temple in the midst of the city, and, if no temple, then no set-apart ministry (Rev. 21:22-26).

In this new city all the nations are welcome, and the gates are never shut, for all the nations will come to worship the "Lord God Almighty and the Lamb." If this plan for unity of creation, described in other metaphors in Ephesians, is the goal of our life in the church, then our work of ministry is work that needs to be carried out on behalf of all God's creation and not in communities cut off from service to the world. In the same way, those who carry out this ministry do so in the hope that one day they will be "going out of business." The ministry into which they were all ordained at baptism will become in reality what it was always in the process of becoming, a service of Christ's freedom in which all are invited to take part.

In this time of anticipation of God's future, we have an opportunity to live as if that New Creation were part of our lives by removing the divisions between ourselves and others, and sharing in Christ's ministry. In doing this, we will be on the way to educating for partnership by being a *community of learning* where building up is taking place. In the midst of such a community the ferment of Christ's presence will continually push us beyond all the commas and the false divisions so that, together with Christ, we become a *community of freedom.*

3

EDUCATION AS EXODUS

While he was studying at Yale Divinity School, David Drake took a leave of absence to live on a kibbutz in Israel. He wrote of his journey as follows:

> And there is a third and stranger kind of learning, one that involves not filling up or building up, but tearing down and emptyings. . . . The burnt-out ghettoes of your prejudices and expectations must be cleared away without pity to the foundations. The vessels which held the knowledge of your own culture must be drained, and the dregs poured out. Then, when you are hungry and thirsty and long for a roof over your head, someone from work invites you to their house for coffee and cakes and explains in broken English that you are welcome like a member of the family. The romance of your own sorrow and alienation is the last illusion to be swept away. You step out new-born into another culture; now you can begin to learn.[1]

Education for partnership happens as we become partners together, not only in a community of learning but also in a community of freedom where our lives are shaped by God into a partnership with and for others. In this chapter the metaphor for education is changed so that the liberating dimension of education for partnership is underlined. Such a dimension was implied in the discussion of "building up" in Chapter 2, but it needs to be underlined here so that we do not forget that *edification involves exodus,* and exodus involves edification. The invitation to become partner is an invitation to share with God as a partner in freedom.

PARTNER IN FREEDOM

"Let us not have any illusions, the way toward the world of tomorrow leads into the desert," writes Hans Hoekendijk. Immediately we know what he means. *We* are on an exodus journey that leads into the desert, a journey that is long, dusty, and difficult. This is not some old musty metaphor that we dust off occasionally for Sunday school pageants with "burning" bushes and cardboard "seas." It is a metaphor for our lives now, as we live out the "already/not yet" of our lives as partners in God's New Creation.

> I believe that the Biblical story of the exodus will, in a very special way, become our story—even if the outcome is different. . . . Where now we only vaguely and uncertainly detect a tract, there will be a path clearly shown us. What happens along the way will not be so conspicuous. Nothing for the newspapers. Here and there a sign of shalom: reconciliation, peace, joy, freedom. A pennyworth of hope for people who have given up hope. A parcel of desert made inhabitable, a bit of life made human by that incorrigible Humanist, who is well pleased with [humankind].[2]

If exodus is our story, then it is in that story that we may find clues about education for partnership in a community of freedom. The story begins and ends with God's action in delivering the people of Israel. Having heard the cries of the people and seen their oppression, God calls Moses to lead the people out of Egypt into the desert and, finally, to the Land of Canaan. The action of God makes the people of Israel covenant partners, for they are to become those who obey this God of justice and liberation. Thus the slaves in Egypt are set free and invited to become a community on its way toward freedom. All who experience God's liberation also become members of this ragtag freedom band, on the way to the Promised Land.

Come to Deliver

In Ex. 3:1-4:17 we find the story of God's appearance to Moses. He is living as a fugitive in Midian when God speaks to him out of the burning bush. He receives a call to be God's partner in the actions of liberation and, in spite of much reluctance on Moses' part, is finally ordered by God to return to Egypt and get on with the task. The story clearly illustrates the general description of partnership we have discussed. Here we find a new focus of relationship between Moses and God, in which there is common commitment to the actions of deliverance and common struggle in the actual exodus and formation of a new social community, within the wider context of the political structures of ancient Egypt and Canaan.

The narrative as it now stands is woven together out of several strands of tradition. Of particular interest in our quest to understand God's action in creating a community of freedom is Ex. 3:7-17, God's "invitation" to share in the work of deliverance. In this section we seem to have material from the Yahwist literary source, which uses the name Yahweh (LORD in the RSV) for God and identifies the holy mountain on which Moses received the law as Sinai (vs. 7-8, 16-17). We also have material from the source called Elohist, which uses the name Elohim (God in the RSV) for God and knows the holy mountain as Horeb (vs. 9-15). In vs. 7-12, Moses is told that God has begun to deliver the people and commissioned them to go to Pharaoh. In vs. 13-17, Moses objects to the task and seeks a sign from God to verify God's promise.

The narrative presents God's *freedom for* the people as the ground of their confidence, and, ultimately, of their deliverance from slavery. In the exodus story the liberating action of God produces a covenant partnership in which the people of Israel promise to obey the commandments of the One who is a faithful liberator. The freedom of God is portrayed as the ground of all human freedom and of the ability to relate in partnership. Because God reaches out beyond Godself to the people, they are able to respond in reaching out beyond themselves in partnership with God and others. Freedom is understood not only as an accumulation of social, political, economic, and personal benefits but, even more importantly, as a gift of God that provides a horizon of hope for all life. The Israelite community came to know that the source of their life was the One who was free for them. Their hope was founded on the liberating action of God, already experienced at the Red Sea, and then experienced over and over again in the events of their lives. In the same way today Christians in the midst of struggle and suffering also ground their hope in the liberation already accomplished by the deliverance of Jesus Christ from the social and personal powers of sin and death.[3]

Because of the nature of freedom as a gift, it can never be defined once and for all. Freedom defined is freedom no longer, as it always transcends all our definitions and concepts. Freedom can only be described as it is actualized in an event of liberation, and this is what is going on in our exodus narrative. The story of God's freedom for Israel is told and celebrated with us so that the word *exodus* ("going out") becomes much more than a name for the second book of Moses. It comes to have the meaning of freedom itself, so that when we speak of the freedom of God, we speak of a journey. Thus the Hebrews described the keeping of the revealed will of God in the law as "walking," and the early Christians spoke of their faithful response to the resurrection event as "walking worthy" of their calling (Eph. 4:1, KJV).[4] To be set free is to be set on a journey of obedience, going out together with others and for others toward God's future.[5]

God delivered the people and thus they all became partners in the process. They all had to play their part and to pay the price of freedom. They had to be willing to join in the freedom struggle, to confront Pharaoh, and to journey in a desert if need be, keeping on going in God's work of putting things right. Those who responded to God's act were not just the leaders we know, such as Moses, Aaron, and Miriam. Nor were they what the RSV translates literally as "sons of Israel," in Ex. 3:10-11. They were all the Israelite slaves—men, women, and children who probably joined with other groups of oppressed people in the Land of Canaan. They all had to make the journey, and we hear of much murmuring and hankering after the imagined luxuries of the "fleshpots" of Egypt once they found themselves having to live out the continuing price of freedom (Ex. 16:1-3). Out of the exodus there emerged a new social reality, a *community of freedom*. As Walter Brueggemann describes it:

The participants in the Exodus found themselves, undoubtedly surprisingly to them, involved in the intentional formation of a *new social community* to match the vision of *God's freedom.* That new social reality, which is utterly discontinuous with Egypt, lasted 250 years.[6]

The people who acknowledged that God had delivered them became a community of freedom which remembered that their very existence as a people depended on God's initiative in caring about them. In response they were committed to care for the marginalized, oppressed people of society and to live by the laws of their covenant partner.

Israel had difficulty learning to be a freedom community. They had to learn that liberation from oppression also included a new way of life in freedom for community and mutual responsibility.[7] And what about those of us who do not experience oppression in such dramatic forms? How can we learn to be part of a freedom community? How can we share in the story of exodus as good news? Certainly the details of our deliverance and response will be quite different. Dorothee Soelle has suggested that those who live in affluent nations and societies need to develop a theology of liberation for those dwelling among the "fleshpots of Egypt."[8] This is an important task if we are to find a *pedagogy for the oppressor* that will assist in the building up of a freedom community in that context. God sets us free from the structures of oppression and domination in our society, but we do not always want to be set free if those structures benefit us. Nor do we always want to respond to a call to obedience with a new life-style and standard of living that contributes to the liberation of neighbor and nature. The road to freedom never has been easy for any one person or any group. Yet it is a road we must take if we are going to educate for partnership together in God's actions.

The Sign for You

Moses certainly did not find his task particularly easy. The tradition tells us that, like most prophetic figures in the Bible, he had been prepared for his role in a mysterious way unknown to him until his call. He was an ideal leader of a revolt because he was born a Hebrew slave, but brought up as an Egyptian prince. He was what sociologists call *status inconsistent*, an upper-class person who didn't belong there.[9] Because of this he would be more able to see the need for social change, and to make good use of his experience in Pharaoh's court and as a desert fugitive. As the narrative presents Moses, he wasn't reluctant just because he felt inadequate for the task or was unwilling to pay the cost. Moses was also not sure that God would deliver the people. The various refusals and objections on his part may once have come from different sources, but they now serve to heighten the drama of his call and the difficulty of the task.

In Ex. 3:1-17 the thing that strikes us is that, although Moses asks for a sign, in neither case is the sign that is given unambiguous. In fact, the wording in v. 12 does not even make clear whether or not a sign was given. Some scholars, such as Martin Noth, even argue that the sign was lost when the editor combined the two different literary accounts.[10] Others say that the sign will be the future confirmation when the Israelites gather to worship as a free people on the holy mountain. Brevard Childs argues that the ambiguity of the sign is due to confusion about the type of pattern of prophetic call being followed in the narrative. Sometimes a prophet is portrayed as receiving a sign that the call is true by an actual event that prefigures what is promised (Jer. 44:29). At other times the sign is an extraordinary event that does not prefigure the future (I Sam. 10:1). Childs says that the sign indicated in Ex. 3:12 is of the latter type. The extraordinary event of the burning bush has been misplaced in the text and appears before God's commission rather than in the usual place at the end of the prophetic commission.[11]

Moses is given a task to perform and he is not sure that God's power will carry it through. In order to convince the people that he has word from a God who is known to be faithful and powerful, Moses asks for a second type of sign. He asks for God's identity or name (Ex. 3:13-17). According to Von Rad,

> the subject is in the name, and on that account the name carries with it a statement about the nature of its subject or at least about the power appertaining to it.[12]

In the Elohist tradition this is the moment when the proper name of God is revealed. Up to this event the source uses Elohim ("gods") as the general name for God. The Yahwist, however, has already been using the name Yahweh and simply indicates the identity of the Lord as the God of Abraham, Isaac, and Jacob (3:16). The Elohist tells us that the divine name is "I AM WHO I AM" (3:14). The answer is not so much a refusal to answer or to give a sign as an indication of the nature of the God who is faithful and yet *free from* human attempts to control or manipulate God's power.

There is no exact agreement about what the divine name Yahweh means. It seems to have been an abbreviated form of a sentence name for the divine. The theory of William Albright, developed by Frank Cross, is that it evolved from the name "El who creates the (armed) hosts." Gottwald says,

> the causative verb *yahwi* became the proper name Yahweh as the historico-social action of El in bringing the mutant Israelite intertribal society into being was singled out as the primary function of deity.[13]

That is, Yahweh became known as the Creator God who created not only the hosts of heaven but also the power of the new Israelite society. As in the earlier sign, the answer is most clear in the light of later events. Yahweh was the one who brought Israel into existence, and the giving of the name celebrates that fact.

Some of the ambiguity of the prophetic signs has to do with the ambiguity of prophetic truth, which depends on God for its verification. When Spirit-filled men and women spoke God's word, the word was most likely to be remembered as true word when it actually came to pass (Jer. 28:7-9). The truth of their message depended on a *critical* consciousness of the continuity and discontinuity of the present life of the community with that of God's will for covenant faithfulness among the people. James Sanders has pointed out that true prophets were able to distinguish whether a particular historical hour called for words of comfort or judgment.[14] They spoke from within their *community* and to that particular setting, pointing to the memory of God's mighty acts of redemption as the sign of *commitment* to covenant faithfulness. Yet, like Moses, they had to live with the ambiguities and personal, social, and political problems of that *context*. They often found themselves inadequate for the task of partnership with God, yet compelled by the power of God's Spirit to speak and act.

Israel had no proof that God would act as liberator in the midst of the people. As Abraham Heschel has said: "There are no proofs for the existence of the God of Abraham. There are only witnesses." [15] To the "nonperson," God's action at the Red Sea was enough. "No people" had become "God's people," and *exodus* was their witness to the One who had created them as a community of freedom (Hos. 2:23). This witness was often costly, for liberation was a sociopolitical process as well as a gift of grace. But the people were never alone. There was a "faithful and true" Partner who said, "And this will be a sign for you. . . . I will be with you" (Rev. 19:11; Luke 2:12; Ex. 3:12).

EDUCATION AND EXODUS

In the Hebrew-Christian tradition, *exodus* has become the name of our freedom journey. Whether we point to the freedom experienced at the Red Sea or in the resurrection of Jesus Christ, we still understand our freedom as a gift from God who redeems us from personal and societal bondage, reclaiming us as partners in New Creation. *Education* can also be seen as a journey toward freedom and wholeness. This is not an unfamiliar metaphor for education in general, which is spoken of as a process of self-development toward wholeness. For instance, Dwayne Heubner of Teachers College, Columbia University, has described it as a

> search for communities by groups of people on pilgrimage working the land with their tools, building the structures that house them from the elements, caring for those who are pushed into their presence, reshaping their life together, and telling and retelling the stories of where they have been and where they seem to be going. [16]

Viewing education in this way may help us to see more clearly the relationship of liberation theologies and education.

Theology and Education

The relationship of theology and education is a perennial problem, not only for those who write books on the theory of Christian education but also for those who want faith to shape the lives of learners and teachers in their churches. Frequently Christian educators try to solve the dichotomy between theology and education by defining both components and then adding them together or correlating their meanings. It would seem to me, however, that we might learn to do *education theologically* and *theology educationally* if we avoid separate definitions of the components and make use of a description of the total configuration in which education happens. Both edification and exodus are possible descriptive metaphors for the educational process from the perspective of Christians seeking to understand how to educate for partnership. And they are both descriptions of theology as what Krister Stendahl calls "worrying about what God is worrying about: mending creation."[17] Edification as the partnering process includes both the gift of new life in Christ and growth toward maturity. Exodus as partnership in God's liberating action includes both the gift of liberation and the journey toward freedom.

Frequently the formation of an uneasy synthesis between theology and education is made by relating them as theory and practice. Theology is the abstract theory and education is what you do to get people to learn.[18] Yet it doesn't take much reflection to discover that theology and education each have a wide variety of theories and an equally wide variety of practice. Because of this, some educators try to clarify the confusion by eliminating theology from the discussion of religious education.[19] Others are caught in the trap of thinking that when we have our theology straight (orthodox?), education will be an automatic result.[20] Of course, both approaches simply operate with unexamined assumptions about the part of the task that they choose to ignore. Often the result is what some would call "bad theology" and others would call "bad education."

The relationship of theory and action is always a problem, even within one discipline, let alone two, for no one theory leads directly to any one action. Yet the two always must be brought together in some way. As Freire points out, thinking without action is *verbalism* and action without thinking is *activism*.[21] One way of relating the two is to relate them in an ongoing process of action-reflection-action, so that the two are always correcting and informing each other.[22] Looked at in this way, both theology and education would be a dynamic and open-ended process of continuing action and reflection. The biblical metaphor for this journey of faith that relates particularly well to the emphasis on the freedom dimension of education and theology is that of the exodus. In this journey metaphor *educare*, meaning to raise children, or lead out, is exploded into *exodus*, going out together as part of God's freedom movement.[23] In this perspective there is much that theology and education have in common, especially when that theology includes action and reflection on the meaning of liberation.

Education and theology as academic disciplines are not always associated with liberation. Education is often viewed as a process of enculturation or socialization into a particular culture. And, just as often, theology is viewed as analysis of the origins and teachings of a religious community.[24] In this perspective the disciplines contribute to maintaining the status quo in society, continuing the oppression of those already at a disadvantage because of racism, sexism, and classism. In this sense theology and education need to be liberated to serve people on their journey together toward freedom.

This need for a *new style of theology* was made dramatically clear to me at a small United Presbyterian conference of women about "Theological Reflections on Liberation" which I attended a few years ago. Several of the women declared adamantly that they would *not do theology!* For them, theology was a tool for marginalizing women in the church. Women were kept in their inferior place by the so-called logic of the experts who supported the way things were by giving expert footnotes to the teachings of the church. This was a particularly difficult message for me to hear, because I had found theology as practiced in my parish in East Harlem so exciting and liberating that I had gone to school to become a teacher of theology! Ever since, an important purpose of my work has been to find ways in which theology and education can be experienced as a source of liberation in people's lives.

This can happen when theology reflects on the biblical themes of exodus and resurrection. These themes about God's ongoing action in the "mending of creation" provide the foundation of liberation theologies that are written out of the experience of oppression in the light of partnership in God's liberating actions of bringing about New Creation.[25] When theology begins with our own experience of the biblical story of slavery, exodus, wandering, and hope, we are all invited to "show and tell" what God has done, and thus become partners in theology.

Such partnership is strengthened by the style of liberation theologies which encourages people to participate in the process, sharing the actions and thoughts of their lives. This style of doing theology is a *collective* attempt to live out our faith, and all are invited to take part. In the *commitment* to justice there is a sharing of God's bias toward the poor and marginalized who listen for good news (Matt. 11:15). Such a style is *contextual*, moving inductively out of particular situations and experiences to understand the meaning of God's summons to journey with others toward freedomland. In this journey *critical* reflection and action is important to those who are seeking to discern the Way.

A *new style of education* is equally important. For it too is often a tool of oppression in our churches and society. It serves the economic interests of our society by preparing persons to fit into the system or giving a rationale for their rejection by the system that does not need them. For instance, the high rate of dropouts in city high schools is a result of a clear message from the educational system that many of the students are not good enough and "deserve to fail" in school and in jobs. Yet education can be a process of liberation or exodus when it is seen as a partnership with others in the journey toward God's intended wholeness. Such education as exodus could contribute to the goal of educational ministry as a process of coming to critical and committed awareness of ourselves and the world in the light of God's intended purpose for New Creation.

Education as exodus would have a style similar to that of

liberation theologies and would carry out the same style as the prophetic witness of Moses and the biblical prophets. It would invite both teachers and students to take part in a *collective* style in which the community learns as it goes forward on the exodus journey together, learning from one another along the way. The experience of God's liberation would shape the *commitment* of those who have been through the waters of baptism and themselves struggle to "not be conformed . . . but transformed" (Rom. 12:2). The learning would begin where people are in their own *context* and yet seek to include the insights of all those who know what it means to be marginalized and oppressed so that we can better understand the cost of slavery and the gift of freedom. In developing *critical* and committed awareness, education as exodus would encourage people to continue their journey of doubt and faith as people of God's covenant and promise.

It is difficult to spell out what exodus as education might look like in any one setting, be it in a community of resistance and struggle, a church community, or an educational institution. We need to live out such a journey together with others in order to celebrate the successes and defeats by sharing our stories and the biblical stories. For instance, we might tell of how we enhanced the partnership of all ages in worship by emphasizing communal style in children's sermons. When the children gave their own sermons through plays, song, and actions, everyone joined in and "got the message."[26] Or we might tell about a theology course in which the participants were encouraged to do critical reflection on ministry in the organizations for social change where they had field placements. Sometimes the reflection was critical enough to get them fired![27] Or we might describe house Bible study groups which began, not with the reading of the text, but with "show and tell" about concerns that people brought to share with each other in the midst of biblical reflection.[28] Whatever our stories, they would be describing ways people come to consciousness of their partnership in God's liberating actions by sharing in a community of freedom.

Consciousness of Partnership

In turning to look more closely at how consciousness

develops, we can make use of the discussion of partnership development in Chapter 2. A community of support is important so that persons can risk failure and be encouraged to grow in being partners. Persons also need a variety of experiences in a wider context that exposes them to other perspectives and provides opportunities for entering into a variety of roles and relationships. Cognitive conflict can also be promoted by exposure to significant others who model more mature values of cooperation. Critical consciousness of the need for partnering actions grows through the caring and challenge of those who wish to be partners in learning and in freedom. An important aspect of this changed consciousness is the changed actions that go with it, and opportunities are needed for persons to test out their changing commitments by actions of social action and service.

The style of development most helpful to growth in partnership is that of interdependence. But all the other styles of dependence, counterdependence, and selfdependence are also important to the communal process of growth and change that in turn encourages participants to grow. The aim of examining such psychological styles of development is not simply to learn how people's lives are shaped through interaction with other persons and the wider society.[29] Such shaping, often called *socialization*, is described from a sociological perspective by Peter Berger as a process in which human beings create their social reality by interacting with their environment, and then in turn are shaped by that social reality and the language and symbols which give it meaning.[30] The aim of our examination is to identify points at which persons may be helped to become conscious of the contradictions and inconsistencies of various views of the world, including their own. A critical consciousness is crucial to the development of partnership as a new focus of relationship in which persons come to see all of reality out of a perspective of critical commitment to Christ and to the reality of God's New Creation.

Such growth in consciousness of the need for partnership is very similar to what Paulo Freire and other Latin-American writers call *conscientization*. Conscientization is learning to perceive the social, political, economic, racial, and ecclesial contradictions and to take steps together with others to change them.[31] This process of learning what is really going on in our social world by looking beneath the rhetoric at the basic problems and social injustices is different from that of the developmental stages of Fowler and Kohlberg. It is a description of intentional consciousness-raising and its hoped-for results. In addition, the changes of consciousness are viewed as springing from changed actions as well as perceptions, and are understood as a spiral process in which persons often repeat or skip phases. Yet the phases can be discerned as a dialectic of liberation in which persons become aware of the reality of freedom as a problem and a possibility in their lives.[32]

Persons may be unaware of the reality of systemic oppression and the possibility of liberation in their lives because they are so chained that to move is suicide, or so privileged that, like the young Buddha, they seem not to know that suffering and death exist. However, most persons are aware of the social structures of oppression in which the fabric of society continues to discriminate against persons because of sex, race, poverty, sexual preference, age, etc.[33] They are also aware of the ferment of freedom that causes oppressed groups to resist this denial of their human need to be treated as a subject and not an object, and to participate together with others in shaping an open future.

The spiral of conscientization begins with oppressed groups interpreting their reality from the perspective of the so-called *happy slave*. Here persons protest that they are happy as they are, be that as an uneducated Appalachian coal miner or an overeducated housewife. Such protest is related to a very rational fear of change; when the power structures are stacked against them, the subordinate persons are the most likely to be hurt when change is attempted. This is what Jean Baker Miller calls "rigged" conflict, "one conducted solely in terms set by others, terms that guarantee that women (or blacks, or poor . . .) will lose."[34] This is why Moses did not want to take on Pharaoh. It was guaranteed that the Israelite slaves would lose, except for God's meddling with the social reality! Members of oppressor groups at the same phase of consciousness will tend to use the "joke style." Here they try, a little nervously, to pretend that their dominant position is not being questioned, by making bad jokes about "uppity women" or "lazy blacks."

This type of consciousness that resists change gives way to *emulation of the oppressor* as the subordinate persons seek their own equality on the basis of the social standards set for success by the dominant group. One important form of this for women and blacks is educational certification which is supposed to give them equal access with white males to jobs. Like Moses, they strive to grow up in Pharaoh's household! The dominant groups move to what is called the "liberal expert" style. They know all the sociological data and have learned some of the new language and cultural styles. This enables them to retain control of the social situation by defining the situation and the problems and deciding how to "make affirmative action work" or explaining what it is "that women need."

The style of emulation does not succeed in eliminating systemic oppression, because the social system itself, quite apart from the actions of any one person, will make it difficult for subordinates to be accepted as equal and will make it impossible for an entire group such as blacks in the United States to overcome the basic structures of racism. This would require more than changes in any one area such as education, employment, housing, or health. It would require a basic change in the rules of the whole system and in the way the dominant group views and interprets the social reality of the nation. Thus when persons or groups find that education, hard work, or middle-class values do not make things equal, they move individually or collectively into *rage*. Through anger, or crying, or self-destructive behavior such as riots, or horizontal violence against persons of their own group, the whole rigged game is rejected.[35] Dominant groups in this phase take on the style of "righteous anger." They proclaim that the other groups marginal to the power of society did not follow the right game plan prescribed by the liberals and now have gotten out of hand. Blaming the victims for their victimization, they bring in more police in the case of riots; send persons off to a psychiatrist in the case of uncontrollable wives; or send slaves off to the desert if they have been bringing plagues on the land.

With the support of other persons who share these experiences but themselves are, at least in part, what Kohlberg calls "one step ahead," oppressed groups and persons may begin to seek out their own *cultural identity*. The energy of their rage is channeled into the search for a past that will be usable in shaping a new identity and a new future. They identify with their own past and with that of their own group, valuing its cultural heritage and celebrating its history. They seek strength for the continuing journey to freedom, as did Israel long ago, from the story of liberation struggles, be they "slaves in revolt" or "suffragettes on the march." New heroes and stories are discovered and shared in a search for self-identity in a usable past that contradicts the dehumanizing view and actions experienced in society. Some persons who benefit from structures of oppression also move into the "identity" phase and begin to search their own history to find out what went wrong with a culture that is destructive of the basic needs of many of their sisters and brothers around the globe.[36] As we shall see in Chapters 5 and 6, it is at this stage that oppressor groups begin to need a pedagogy that will assist them in the struggle to change, and oppressed groups need one that can help them "keep on keepin' on" the freedom journey.

Out of such a continuing search to understand the causes of oppression and to develop new styles of mutual interdependence comes the possibility of *partnership* in which there is a dynamic interrelationship as groups and persons move into a pattern of cooperation toward common goals or objectives. These relationships are not necessarily equal, but they can provide the possibility of temporary inequality so that groups know that their future is open-ended. This style of interdependence is built out of a consciousness of the position of other persons that is open to dialogue and takes seriously their views of reality and their social needs.

A typology of coming to consciousness of partnership through a dialectic of liberation is not intended to be a set of stages for educational curriculum. It can inform our educational thinking about partnership, but it is too "messy" for any set of "graded" curriculum materials. It represents an organic process of changing consciousness which moves in a spiral. We often find ourselves in more than one phase at a time as well as participants in structures of oppression in both dominating and subordinated roles. In the case of women the conflict of consciousness is increased because, like Moses, they are often status inconsistent, benefiting from the privilege of the dominant class, yet still belonging to a subordinate group. Groups and individuals often return to earlier perceptions in the face of conflict and vulnerability. Riots and rage do not happen just once, nor do relationships always turn into or remain partnerships. What the typology does underline, however, is some important clues for exploring education for partnership through sharing with others in the community of freedom.

The first clue is that consciousness of partnership relates to *all the phases* of conscientization, for they are all phases of changing understanding of social reality and changing style of action on the freedom journey. Secondly, the movement toward a consciousness of partnership is facilitated in every phase by those who are willing to be *partners* on the journey, especially those who have already moved ahead and can show others the way. A third clue is that one can educate for partnership only by *beginning where persons are* and trying to be partner there. This is important for our awareness of our own position and that of others when trying to find a common agenda around which to work. A fourth discovery is that full partnership and interdependence is a phase that becomes possible *on the other side of liberation*. Persons have to see their reality from a consciousness of equal human dignity and strength in order to find a new focus of relationship in partnership. Lastly, in this continuing process the clues concerning God's New Math in Chapter 1 are important for keeping the process going. Especially important might be the need for a "third thing" or commitment to action together that provides a way for unequals to make a mutual commitment about something they care about equally. Keeping roles and responsibilities flexible through "temporary inequality" would be important as well as the practice of "calculated inefficiency" by those who seek to provide room for others to grow as their partners.

This typology, like all such artificial descriptions, is

oversimplified. Yet, as we look at the events of black liberation, women's liberation, and other liberation movements in the 1960's and 1970's we can see such shifts at work. As we look at those events we can also see that changing consciousness and action is no utopia, for the journey is long and the horizon of freedom continually moves ahead of us. Many of us have also experienced such changes of consciousness in our own lives as well. One student at Yale in a Clinical Pastoral Education program reflected on the experience of such a change over the period of a year by describing her conversion from "competition" to "partnership." She had spent her life trying to be better than others, seeking approval from important others by getting good grades in school. She found that this familiar competitive self-identity was no help to her in a ministry with persons sick and dying in the hospital. This caused "cognitive conflict" in which her view of reality did not work and needed to change. As she began to sense the contradictions, she found support from a community that did not reject her in the midst of personal crisis. The Clinical Pastoral Education group responded to her tentative reaching out by reaching out in return and by providing a framework for analyzing and naming the situation in order to change it. Thus her educational experience became one of partnership rather than performance.[37]

Education for partnership in God's liberating actions is often education that takes place intentionally in contexts where persons are challenged to grow and change, be they schools, communities, families, or work settings. In recognition of this, more and more programs for adults are being designed as *education by extension*. The university, seminary, or continuing education center designs the programs so that they take place in the life setting of a group of pastors or laypersons by bringing resources and teachers to that setting. Such is the basis of the Master of Arts in Human Values designed for laypersons by San Francisco Theological Seminary. It is also the pattern for more and more of the theological education in the Third World where persons are educated as pastors while continuing their work and family life. This type of education sees life itself as part of the process and seeks to provide tools for critical theological and social reflection helpful to the journey toward freedom rather than to shape persons into the model of academic learning.[38]

Education as exodus is education that equips us for continuing discovery of the Way along the road. Like the Israelites of old, communities of freedom today look for a prophetic ministry that will facilitate this form of learning. Biblical tradition tells us that the Israelite people being formed into a new social reality were forced to new levels of consciousness about their partnership with Yahweh as well as with one another. Their struggle to become covenant partners in an egalitarian society, distinct from the hierarchical societies of their Egyptian and Canaanite neighbors, was supported by prophetic leaders such as Moses, Joshua, and Deborah who provided continuing critical discernment of their *real* situation before God.

PROPHETIC MINISTRY

Prophetic ministry is not different from educational ministry. Rather, they are both dimensions of the same ministry of Jesus Christ, who sets us free to become partners with others in service. In the discussion of educational ministry in Chapter 2, I underlined the communal dimension of ministry. The community is built up in faith as a sign of New Creation through the gifts of confidence in God's love and faithfulness; and knowledge of the story of that faithfulness in Jesus Christ, shared in a community of learning. It is also built up through the gift of consent or commitment to live out that story in our own lives as partners in a community of freedom.

The implication of this is that education for partnership calls for a variety of persons willing to be partners, and not for just one SUPER-EDUCATOR who is able to be teacher, pastor, and prophet all at once. It does not even call for a SUPER-CHURCH which is able to be a community of faith, learning, and freedom all at once and all the time. The basis of the community's ministry is God's action in Jesus Christ through which we are already set free and called into partnership. The gifts of the Spirit provide a variety of gifts as we struggle on our desert journey to become what we already are, partners. The expectation that one day our koinonia in Christ will be completed in the New Creation keeps us on the way. Along the way the ministry of teaching-pastors and prophets is needed. Because this ministry will often come from a variety of persons, the special gift needed by those seeking to educate for partnership is not necessarily prophecy or teaching, but the humble expectation that both are present in the midst of the community, and the expectant humility to seek out those gifts for the "equipment of the saints" as we move along *the way toward tomorrow.*

Community of Freedom

Prophetic ministry is never separate from the community of freedom where it is practiced. As we saw in the discussion of the prophetic ministry of Moses, the tasks are related to the formation and continuing reformation of an Exodus community.[39] Reflection on God's actions of deliverance and covenant faithfulness in the light of the present context of the community lead to a message which often comforts the afflicted and afflicts the comfortable. The role is one of troublemaker among those who ignore the reality of God's justice.[40] In the words of Walter Brueggemann,

> *The task of prophetic ministry is to nurture, nourish, and evoke a consciousness and perception alternative to the consciousness and perception of the dominant culture around us.*[41]

Prophetic ministry has a future dimension in words and actions of justice and service that point to God's intended future. Yet, because it springs out of a community and speaks to that particular community and its present context, the prophetic ministry always points to action needed in the present. But such ministry is not reducible either to foretelling the future or to social action.[42] Its primary gift is the ability to discern God's intention for the community and to promote the development of critical awareness of this call to discipleship among the members of the community.

The way in which we participate in this prophetic task is through education as exodus. Here the process of coming to critical awareness or consciousness of partnership with God, others, and with all creation is intentionally fostered.

Partnership development of the community makes possible a recognition of interdependence and of the need for mutual action on behalf of equality, justice, and a sustainable society. Partnership consciousness grows in a dialectic of liberation as persons are challenged and disturbed, yet welcomed in the tasks of "mending creation." Prophetic ministry helps to clarify God's intention for full partnership in a world groaning for liberation by sharing both words and actions that seek to change the shape of the social reality that fosters division and oppression.

One important example of education as exodus is the rapid expansion of Popular Christian Communities in Latin America. These "basic Christian communities" (*comunidades de base*) provide much of the grass roots organization in the Roman Catholic Church as it seeks to become an advocate for liberation in the face of social, political, and economic repression in Latin America. The formation of such local communities within larger parishes was encouraged by the Second Episcopal Conference at Medellín in 1968 as part of its commitment to identify with the needs of the poor.[43] These groups of ten or twenty persons meeting once or twice a month to read the Bible, to reflect and act together, and to become a community are estimated to number about eighty thousand in Brazil, with another eighty thousand in Spanish-speaking Latin Ameria.[44]

In their quiet and often undramatic life together, these communities form the backbone of the teaching, pastoral, and prophetic ministry of many churches. According to one of the organizers of such groups, José Marins, their purpose is to renew and build Christian community through liturgy, theological reflection, and nurture in the faith. The groups provide a basis for:

Human self-development in Christ in which people:
—are conscious of their dignity; understanding and transforming their universe in a personal way
—live in solidarity and growing/community/with others
—are participating responsibly in the orientation of their lives and the destiny of their community.[45]

Edification takes place in a setting where everyday events

are an occasion for living out the biblical promise by participating in God's liberating actions. For instance, in Vitória, Brazil, five hundred communities collected signatures in a successful petition for expanded bus service so people could get to work. Another community in Recife, Brazil, was able to organize seventeen families in order to resist the needless bulldozing of their shanty town homes.[46]

In meeting these and many other physical, social, and spiritual needs, the Popular Christian Communities are led not only by priests or nuns but also many laywomen and laymen whose gifts of ministry are recognized and developed in these communities, even when they are not recognized within the church hierarchy. The role of the "basic ecclesial communities" in the ministry of learning and freedom can be clearly seen in a recent statement by an ecumenical gathering of Third World theologians who met in São Paulo, Brazil, to discuss "Ecclesiology of Popular Christian Communities."

> The Christian communities—through consciousness-raising, popular education, and the development of ethical and cultural values—exercise among the poor a liberating ministry that is an integral part of their specific mission of evangelization, prophecy, pastoral care, and administering the sacraments.[47]

The Way Toward Tomorrow

Freedom is a journey with others for others, toward God's future. That promised future is our tomorrow. It moves ahead of us on our journey like the cloud and pillar of fire (Ex. 13:21). Our assurance of that future is anchored in the past events of God's liberating action that have already made us partners in the journey and sent us on our way. The prophetic ministry of the community points not only to this assurance but also to God's tomorrow. It criticizes the present reality in the light of what God intends for the world and embodies that intention by acts of justice and liberation now. In a sense it is ministry viewed and practiced from the other end.

Education for partnership in such communal ministry begins with our baptism into Christ's ministry of service and continues through our entire lives. Out of the waters of baptism we have been liberated into the new humanity of which the prophets spoke. Already we are able to live as partners beyond barriers of sex, race, and social status (Gal. 3:28; I Cor. 12:13). The gift of the Spirit allows us to share in prophetic ministry. Our partnership together in God's liberating actions prepares us to be ready to give account of our hope for tomorrow when the moments of witness arise. Such a moment arose in 1977 for four women in Bolivia. The day after Christmas they took their fourteen children to the archbishop's headquarters and began a hunger strike. They were demanding the return and reinstatement of their husbands, who had been fired from the mines and deported, leaving their families destitute. They were also supporting the demand of the churches and other groups for general amnesty for twenty thousand Bolivian political exiles. Although all strikes were against the law, the women decided to underline the Christmas message of justice and peace on earth with their own prophetic sign. Other Christians offered to substitute for the children so they would not die of hunger. The mothers allowed the children to be fed, although they kept them with them and pointed out that the children would soon die in the mines in any case.

The government finally arrested the women and those who had joined the hunger strike in other cities around the country. But an international ecumenical commission had arrived to investigate human rights violations and the archbishop of La Paz also took action. He declared that all the churches in the city would be closed in protest. After twenty-one days of hunger strike the negotiations led to a proclamation of general amnesty and to the return of the exiles. Esther and Mortimer Arias describe this "sign" in *The Cry of My People*:

> They were able to give an example, to risk their lives and the lives of their children when nobody dared to challenge the dominating powers—to challenge Christians and churches and finally to prevail over the apparently unconquerable power of a dictatorship that ruled the country with an iron hand, unchallenged for eight years.[48]

The ministry of the women and their children was a prophetic sign to their own people and to churches and nations. Their partnership in God's liberating actions was the basis of education for partnership. And in their action we see a *new thing:* that the exodus itself is an educational event. Not only are we to understand education as exodus, but also *exodus as education,* for on the journey we learn to be partner.

Let us not have any illusions, the way toward the world of tomorrow leads into the desert. I believe that the Biblical story of the exodus will, in a very special way, become our story— even if the outcome is different.[49]

4

THEOLOGY AS ANTICIPATION

Sometimes your former professors turn out differently from the way you expect! Such is the case of the late Cyril Richardson, who became ever more radical in relation to women's issues as he neared retirement. As professor of church history and Dean of Graduate Studies, Richardson was a *patriarchal* figure at Union Seminary in New York. Yet he moved into a new field of research, working on *matriarchal* figures of the early church. In the light of his new interest I took courage and invited him to tea. We had a great time talking about our feminist projects. Letting the tea get cold, we got into a heated argument about whether feminists could develop a biblically based theology in the light of the ways the Bible is used to legitimatize the inferiority of women and the superiority of men.[1]

The conversation was ended when our respective spouses got hungry for dinner, but the question led me to begin my theological explorations from the other end of the biblical story. By beginning with God's intention for New Creation, a theology of anticipation can help us grow in our ability to anticipate new relationships of partnership in our thinking and action. The basis of such theology is the action of God in bringing about a *great reversal* of reality as we know it so that things no longer add up logically, but multiply grace-fully as part of God's New Math. The prophets help us to think about this new reality clearly and to interpret it imaginatively for our own context.

GOD'S GREAT REVERSAL

Although the words of Jer. 31:15-17 and 31-34 speak to a political situation seven hundred years removed from that of the exodus, there is great similarity in their message for the oppressors and the oppressed. God "remembers" the people of Israel and Judah, and is in the process of bringing about a reversal of the present social and political reality. As one of the reforming prophets of the eighth and seventh centuries, Jeremiah had much to say about the way in which the egalitarian society established in covenant with Yahweh had been denied. Walter Brueggemann points out that by the time of Solomon's kingdom, the politics of oppression, the economics of affluence, and the establishment and control of religion had a very strong resemblance to Pharaoh's Egypt.[2] The description of Jeremiah's call in 1:18 is an indication of this ministry of prophetic judgment in the last years of the Kingdom of Judah.

> And I, behold, I make you this day a fortified city, an iron pillar, and bronze walls, against the whole land, against the kings of Judah, its princes, its priests, and the people of the land.

Jeremiah's task was to testify to God's holy war against the unfaithful people. Over and over he pleaded with the people to repent and to "let Pharaoh go!" With great sorrow he spoke of doom and destruction for a people who would not listen to God. It was only in the face of defeat and exile for the kingdom of Israel and of Judah that Jeremiah uttered words of "a future and a hope" (29:11).[3]

Two of the passages of consolation collected in Jeremiah 30-31 contain the word "new." One points to the *unexpected* reality of a new creation in which relationships between women and men will be changed:

> For the LORD has created a new thing on the earth:
> a woman protects a man.
>
> (Jer. 31:22)

The other passage speaks of God's action in establishing a *new covenant* involving a basic change of heart, will, and action in relation to God. These two texts both take a very radical view of the possibility of something new. God is not defeated by the destruction of the nation of Israel and Judah, nor by the destruction of the covenant relationship. In God's plan this particular *end* for one nation at the hand of their captors is in fact a new beginning for all of humankind. Second Isaiah describes this new possibility in words to the exiles:

> Remember not the former things,
> nor consider the things of old.
> Behold, I am doing a new thing;
> now it springs forth, do you not perceive it?
> (Isa. 43:18-19)

The two passages from Jeremiah 31 are two separate sayings or oracles of the prophet. The first, in vs. 15-22, is in poetic form and probably comes from the early period of his ministry, as Jeremiah is speaking words of comfort to the northern kingdom of Israel, whom he calls Ephraim. Israel had been defeated by Assyria in 721 and carried away into exile. The second passage, in vs. 31-34, is an oracle of Jeremiah which has been edited into prose form, but still contains the prophetic words of Yahweh's address, ". . . says the LORD." It probably comes from a later period, around the time of the destruction of Jerusalem and the exile of the southern kingdom of Judah in 567.

Expect the Unexpected

The "new thing in the land" which Yahweh is creating is surely a great reversal of anything we have experienced. It raises many questions about how God acts in our lives in mending creation, setting it free from the shackles of bondage and decay (Rom. 8:21). Yet it also makes us begin to think expectantly, and to look for the small reversals already at work in our own experience that demand a change of mind and action as we live out God's new reality in our lives.

The oracle in Jer. 31:15-22 proclaims a great reversal in which "female surrounds man." Phyllis Trible, in her book *God and the Rhetoric of Sexuality,* has pointed out that the oracle begins and ends with words of a woman to a woman and the central section is the words of a man, Ephraim, as he confesses his disobedience. The drama in five voices reminds us that the God who is capable of raising up people out of stones is also capable of finding ways to bring blessing to humanity through both women and men (Matt. 3:9). The drama opens in v. 15 with Rachel, Jacob's wife, weeping from her grave because her children, whom God had chosen as a blessing to the nations, were scattered in exile and destroyed. Next Yahweh consoles her with the improbable message, "There is hope for your future." The voice of her son Ephraim is then heard as he returns and asks for restoration. In response, Yahweh, now imaged as a woman, shows motherly compassion and tender mercy to him.[4]

In vs. 21-22 the prophet speaks, telling the exiles to set up road markers, as they are sent into exile, in order to find their way back home. This is an absurd image, comparable to Hansel and Gretel marking their path through the forest with bread crumbs. Israel had already been in exile for over a hundred years. Yet the voice of Jeremiah is full of urgent impatience at Israel, now portrayed as a dillydallying or turnabout virgin. The people are ashamed of their weakness and defeat. Markers in shifting sand are the least of their worries. Their male warriors have become "as women" unable even to protect their land. There is no hope. Yet the final word comes: "Yahweh has created a new thing in the land: female surrounds a man." Yahweh has joined Rachel in declaring motherly compassion for Israel.[5] Perhaps there is also a hint here that the God who made the warriors to become as women is also capable of making the women powerful enough to protect the warriors.[6] Whatever translation is attempted here (and there are many), something radical is imaged. In words drawn from the creation story of Gen. 1:27, God is pictured as making female, and thus all creation, in a new way.[7]

God's actions here are so unexpected that we can hardly comprehend their meaning or imagine what a creation might look like in which male/female relationships were quite different. But God's actions are often this way. God doesn't begin with our presuppositions, but with presuppositions drawn from the other end of history. God's arithmetic is definitely the new math of great reversals in which small numbers are used to represent the whole, and the marginalized and oppressed turn out to be agents of liberation. In other cases, God increases the numbers when we least expect it, and gifts for the work of new creation multiply like loaves and fishes (Matt. 14:13-21). God's great reversal seems far away from our own lives in this time before the fulfillment of New Creation. In a world full of suffering and exile, the road markers and hints of God's action seem at best to point to a risky path.

To join God in upholding the cause of the poor and needy, in protecting those whom the rulers of Israel and Judah (and of our own land) have marginalized, is not easy, nor is it popular. Yet it is one of the ways that we become involved in *small reversals* that are part of a "new thing" that Yahweh has created in the land. Partnership in God's liberating actions involves us in theology of anticipation. We begin to look for small reversals by thinking from the other end of God's New Creation, and then acting out of this reverse perspective. A clue to this way of thinking is that we should *expect the unexpected!* By this openness to the future we are more likely to hear the words of judgment we need to hear in the midst of comfort as well as the words of hope in situations that appear beyond hope.

Sometimes the reversals are very faint hints, and sometimes they take many years, or many lifetimes. For instance, a hint of reversal in the issue of the ordination of women to ministry and priesthood happened to me when I attended a Consultation of the World Council of Churches on that topic in Strasbourg, in 1979. I went there thinking that we would be doing the same old thing in asking women to justify themselves by proving that they are capable of representing Christ at the altar. I was a bit tired of discussing whether I could do something I had been doing for over twenty years. Or I expected we would be asked to show that we would not be unreasonable in making demands that might jeopardize unity conversations between world confessional bodies, some of whom do not believe that ordination is a justice issue. I was reluctant to travel to France in order to be an "uppity woman." Yet I hoped that something new would happen. At the very least I would learn new things and make new friends (and possibly some new enemies). I discovered to my surprise that there was a hint of a new thing, a small reversal. In theological discussion about the ordination of women, the presence of a large number of women with men tended to shift the conversation. Women did not have to prove themselves, but theologians did! They had to rethink together the nature of ministry as a two-class system of the church and to clarify, not why women, but why anyone should be ordained for life. They had to begin to rethink the meaning of unity at the expense of justice. Here in one small reversal, women stopped being a problem and became an opportunity for a new level of dialogue.

Business of New Covenant

A new social reality such as that envisioned in New Creation calls for the gift of partnership between God and the people. The new covenant described in the oracle of Jer. 31:31-34 envisions this possibility through creation of a new human being, one whose total being is in harmony with God so that God's will is "done on earth" (Matt. 6:9-13). In Jeremiah's view, God's judgment of Israel's sin was total. Their defeat and exile was God's way of declaring that there could be no more "business as usual."[8] The status quo of injustice, greed, and solemn assemblies was finished. The new covenant was no mere update or renewal program. It was God's way of beginning again to create human beings able and willing to do God's will. Just as the first oracle reflects the words of Gen. 1:27 and transforms them, this oracle reflects the Old Testament covenant language, now radically transformed.

In v. 32, Jeremiah speaks of the covenant that God made with the forebears of Israel and Judah on Mt. Sinai. The basis of this covenant or agreement was God's gracious action in delivering the people from Egypt and the confirmation was the people's promise to serve God and to obey the laws delivered to Moses on tablets of stone. Although God continued to be faithful to the covenant relationship, the people of God often denied the covenant by their actions and had to be reminded of their unfaithfulness.[9] Yet the breaking of the covenant is not the last word. God continues to reach out to the people, not only to punish but also to restore the relationship. This time, according to vs. 33-34, there will be a new covenant written on the inmost being of heart, mind, and will. It will no longer be on "tablets of stone" that can be broken (II Cor. 3:2-6). People will want to obey God because their will and God's are one. They will spontaneously pray as did Jesus in the Garden, "Not my will, but thine, be done" (Luke 22:42). The business of teaching, preaching, and theology will become obsolete because everyone will have a deep relationship with God, established by God's love and forgiveness.

In the new covenant God seeks out a means of self-disclosure in which God will be truly and directly *known*, in the Hebrew sense of a unity in relationship of will and obedience.[10] God's Word of promise has been faithful, and the prophets' words have been faithful to that promise. Yet the people have not lived up to the promise. They have engaged in "cheap talk." The covenant, therefore, is not to be one of words, of speaking and listening, but of direct knowledge and shared will.[11] Those who do the truth will know the truth, and this will set them free (John 8:32).

Over and over, prophetic words of judgment remind us that covenant faithfulness is no easy task. To know the Lord is to be united to God in doing justice and righteousness, in upholding the cause of the poor and needy, in protecting those whom society has marginalized.[12] Thus Jeremiah prophesies to Shallum, son of Josiah:

> Do you think you are a king
>   because you compete in cedar?
> Did not your father eat and drink
>   and do justice and righteousness?
>   Then it was well with him.
> He judged the cause of the poor and needy;
>   then it was well.
> Is not this to know me?
>   says the LORD.

> (Jer. 22:15-16)

Nor is one necessarily thanked for taking a stand with God on behalf of the oppressed. Jeremiah himself suffered so greatly from having the words of God's covenant within his being that he even tried to stop prophesying the words of judgment that made him so unpopular (Jer. 20:9). Contemporary examples of the cost of prophecy are painfully clear. For instance, the blood of the martyrs is becoming an ever-present reality in the witness of the church in Latin America. Many of those who witness, such as Archbishop Oscar A. Romero of San Salvador, join the four women in Bolivia in raising up a sign for justice and peace, but at the cost of their lives.[13]

The message seems unmistakable. God's will written on our hearts means doing God's business of caring for humanity and mending creation, and not just business as usual, caring for ourselves. God's will in our being means that we already know ourselves to be empowered by God to work for signs of God's great reversal in our own communities, churches, and across the world. The clue here is that we are to put ourselves *out of business*. Our work of service is to carry out diakonia in which persons find new relationships of justice and wholeness so that service is no longer needed. Our work of teaching is to share the Word so that all may come to know God and to be able to think and act for themselves. Our work of witness is to "put our bodies on the line" as our offering to God (Rom. 12:1). We can dare to think this way because the new covenant has come to pass in the One who also sealed it with his blood (I Cor. 11:12-25). In fulfilling and embodying the law of God in his heart, mind, and will, Jesus Christ became the transformed Ephraim, the transformed virgin Israel, and caught up in himself what God had hoped for him and for us from the beginning.

THINKING FROM THE OTHER END

Thinking out of God's future as we continue to act in the present can produce what we called "advent shock" in Chapter 1: a dis-ease with business as usual and a desire to live out relationships of justice and faithfulness now. Often this maladjustment leads us to reject biblical authority when it is used to legitimate the ways of old creation. Many women find that the biblical message is so hopelessly patriarchal that it cannot provide a basis for feminist theology.[14] For instance, an Interfaith Consultation held at the Union of American Hebrew Congregations in New York had the theme "How to Survive as a Feminist in a Patriarchal Religion." A paper by Sr. Ann Patrick Ware startled many people when she spoke of "starting on a New Track" because Scriptures and church tradition are "unredeemably sexist."[15]

Yet I have no intention of giving up the biblical basis of my theology. With Rosemary Ruether, I would argue that the Bible has a critical or liberating tradition embodied in its "prophetic-messianic" message. In Ruether's view:

> The primary vision of salvation in the Bible is that of an alternative future, a new society of peace and justice that will arise when the present systems of injustice have been overthrown.[16]

The evidence for a biblical message of liberation for women, as for other marginalized groups, is not found just in particular stories about women or particular female images of God such as that in Jer. 31:20. It is found in God's intention for the mending of all creation.[17] The Bible has authority in my life because it makes sense of my experience and speaks to me about the meaning and purpose of my humanity in Jesus Christ. In spite of its ancient and patriarchal world views, in spite of its inconsistencies and mixed messages, the story of God's love affair with the world leads me to a vision of New Creation that impels my life. Thinking from the other end provides a way of continuing prophetic interpretation so that the Word is heard anew in different cultures and subcultures.

Prophetic Interpretation

I am one of those for whom the Bible continues to be a liberating word as I hear it together with others and struggle to live out its story.[18] For me the Bible is *Scripture* because it is also *script*. It is an authoritative witness to what God has done and is doing in and through the lives of people and their history. It is authoritative because those who have responded to God's invitation to participate in God's actions on behalf of humanity find that it becomes their own lived-out story or script through the power of God's Spirit. My particular story is one that was shaped by seventeen years with a poor, racially mixed community of struggle and witness in the East Harlem Protestant Parish in New York City. In such a context, it was clear that the Bible did not have all the answers. Much of what it said seemed inadequate for the problems we faced—for instance, sayings about slavery, or relations of church and government, or divorce (I Cor. 7:21; Mark 12:14; Matt. 19:3).

Yet the Bible continued to speak to us in worship and house Bible study groups, in ministries of education and action. The stories of the Bible were told, compiled, and preserved in the first place because they spoke to the real needs of the communities out of which they grew. Their ability to speak to basic questions of life gave them authority as an authentic word from God and about God that could help shape lives.[19] They continued to speak to our small interracial community in East Harlem, not with answers to issues of poverty, injustice, and racism, but with hope in the midst of oppression that drove us to look for the answers that might contradict that social, political, and economic reality. The Bible, which often records the way God speaks to people in the midst of suffering, despair, exile, and poverty, came alive among a people who continued to look for the "new thing" that the Lord was to create (Jer. 31:22).

For nine years I wrote an illustrated Bible study lectionary which was used in worship and education programs for all ages.[20] The surprising thing was not that people who could hardly read became involved in biblical interpretation and preaching, but that somehow the texts we really lived with and struggled with seemed to speak in ever new ways on our road toward freedom. In my work overseas and in the United States, in colleges, seminaries, and church bureaucracies, and with women's organizations I have had no reason to change my mind about the authority of the Bible. In East Harlem the story of God's concern for humanity showed us that "nobodies" in the eyes of the dominant society could be "somebodies." I still believe this, believe that in God's sight I am not marginal, but, like my black and Hispanic sisters and brothers in East Harlem, I am created by God and called by the biblical word of promise to become what God intends me to be.

Prophetic interpretation of the biblical promise reminds us to expect the unexpected, seeking to live as partners with a God who is free from us as well as for us. As we saw in Chapter 3, the mark of prophetic interpretation was that it was the "right word" for the "right context." In the midst of unfaithfulness Jeremiah's word was of the unexpected nature of God's judgment. In the exile the word was about the equally unexpected nature of God's New Creation. James Sanders quotes Eva Osswald, saying:

> The true prophet must be able to distinguish whether a historical hour stands under the wrath or the love of God.[21]

According to Sanders, prophetic interpretation was employed by Jesus in explaining the Hebrew Scriptures in the light of the Kingdom of God. It continues to be an important means of discerning both the wrath and the love of God. Discernment depends on the context of the covenant community as the word is interpreted in the light of a particular perspective and a particular set of questions. Remembering the story of God's "mighty acts" is a means of anticipating the present and future meaning of a particular biblical text. A crucial issue in the prophetic interpretation is how we find our analogies to the present. Words of comfort in Jeremiah's time, or in the time of Jesus, should be spoken to people in similar circumstances of oppression so that the message continues to point toward God's purpose of redemption for the creation.[22] In this way the biblical message may continue as an authoritative witness to the dealings of God with the people of God.

Partners in Theology

Prophetic discernment is a gift of God's Spirit, but it is a gift that continues to be found in the midst of people seeking to think and act as a community of anticipation. In learning to think together from the other end, we become partners in the process of thinking about God's action in the world. This is not some optional exercise added on to our lives as partners with God and one another. It is part of the very meaning of partnership that we want to live out the common history of Jesus of Nazareth in our lives as a continuing expression of our new identity in Jesus Christ. In developing the *art of anticiption*, we can share in a continuing process of questioning our actions and those of society in the light of the biblical message of New Creation.

Such a process of questioning is important for all theology as it seeks to be critical, consistent, and documented in its work of understanding and interpreting God's active presence in the world. But it is especially important for liberation theologies as they reflect on experiences of oppression in the light of partnership in God's liberating actions. For this particular style of interpretation the discernment of oppression is not sufficient. Action is dependent not only on critical understanding of reality but also on hope-filled discernment of the signs of liberation, the "already/not yet" of God's future. If liberation looks like God's plans for shalom and not for evil, "to give you a future and a hope," then biblical interpretation looks like a search for ways to *anticipate* and live out this liberating future (Jer. 29:11). If liberation is offered by God in Christ to all humanity, then all are invited to give an account of their hope, and biblical interpretation looks like a *partnership* in theology in which all are welcome (I Peter 3:15-16). If liberation is seen in God's special concern for the poor and oppressed, then biblical interpretation looks like the *questions* of those whose story is tied up with the One who is present among the poor (Matt. 25:31-46). If liberation involves a journey toward God's future, then biblical interpretation looks like faithful *actions* that seek to incarnate the exodus story.

The art of anticipation is very important for feminist theology as well, because it provides a basis for a new understanding of humanity as both male and female in community as God's intention for New Creation. Changing consciousness and actions call not only for the liberation of theology but also for the liberation of the Word of God as spoken through the words of men and interpreted in a male-centered, or androcentric, way.[23] In our search for a biblical basis for the new understanding, the art of anticipation points toward the meaning of partnership, or koinonia, in Jesus Christ as a key to interpreting old creation and old covenant. The creation stories are so overlaid with tradition that it is very difficult to liberate them from the Fall.[24] The covenant tradition, so powerful in its context of liberation and exodus, has also come to be interpreted in a legalistic way that binds persons to the old order. Yet, viewed from the other end, both creation and covenant become *new:* symbols of God's gift of life and future that bypass the traditions of men (Matt. 15:1-6). *Tradition* as God's action of handing over Christ into the hands of coming generations and nations is an open-ended process in which the still living and evolving past becomes a memory of the future (Rom. 8:31-32).[25] In God's action of New Creation women and men are already set free to develop new ways of relating to one another, the world, and God. Feminist theology can also then reflect on this possibility for faith that comes to us out of the biblical message.

The art of anticipation is a continuing circle or spiral of interpretation and a continuing attempt to be suspicious of the classist, racist, and sexist bias brought to the biblical interpretation and found in the text itself. This art of anticipation is not simply reflection, but rather it is a way of life in which persons are partners together in reflecting on and acting out the story of God's love affair with the world. When I have shared this continuing way of Bible study with groups of students, professional theologians, or church communities the text has been studied collectively as well as researched and reflected on individually. The aspects of the collective discussion include discussion of the text and context, question, expectation, action, clue, and next questions.

In collective discussion of a passage we begin with the *context* of the text and of our own lives. As a group we listen to the text seeking to discern critically the cultural context of the writers and hearers and of ourselves, and to be suspicious of the bias of that context in the light of the perspective of marginalized groups.[26] There is no way to be completely unbiased in approaching a text. The text is biased toward a particular situation or context, and the interpreters are biased by their own situations. It is important, therefore, to begin by being honest about our own bias and prior commitments, and to test out this perspective in the light of the research and experience of others.

In the interpretation of the Jeremiah 31 passages, for instance, I needed to note not only the context of Jeremiah's words but also the purpose of those who edited them into the Book of Comfort in chs. 30-31. I also needed to consider that I lived in the "bondage of affluence" rather than in exile and that the words of judgment should be heard even as the words of comfort for the victims were celebrated. As a woman I was particularly biased toward a passage that possibly imaged women as warriors, and imaged Yahweh as a woman having compassion for her children. My fantasy of the "new thing" was not so much of the two hundred women who graduated from U.S. military academies for the first time in 1980, but of Superman, overcome by some super Kryptonite ray gun, crumpling into a phone booth and emerging as . . . Lois Lane!

Working as partners in the theological process, we then need to identify the *questions* that provide an interpretive key, breaking open the text so that it draws us into its own quest. Out of our life experience, and especially out of the experience of those crying out from oppression, we seek the questions that should be addressed to the text and to the traditional interpretations of the text. They are not necessarily questions that the text itself asks. Often these are not questions of intellectual assent and of the nonbeliever, but rather questions of hope and of the nonperson. In the Jeremiah passage I was interested in the question of how one thinks from the other end. What would a new creation look like? Certainly not simply like a reversal of sexism, with women being warriors. I was also suspicious of the new covenant text, asking whether this new covenant was really a source of liberation for women or just a new way for church tradition to bind me more closely to its sacramental life as a means of grace.

Sometimes the questions are clarified as we look further at the biblical horizon of *expectation* and the setting of the particular text in the wider story of what Walter Harrelson has called "promise on the way to fulfillment."[27] Beginning from the perspective of prophetic interpretation the passage may point toward other parts of the Bible. It is important to ask what clues about the biblical message of liberation illuminate, modify, contradict, or echo this text and to look at other texts as a source of interpretation. In such a horizon of expectation we often discover that a particular biblical text responds more clearly to the question, For what may we hope? than the question, What should we do? because of its historical setting in the story of salvation, rather than as only a compilation of

doctrines or ethical guidelines. In the first part of this chapter
it is clear that I saw many parallels to Jeremiah in the vision of
a new heaven and a new earth in Isaiah and Revelation. In
addition, the images of covenant pointed to the dimensions of
the covenant tradition in the story of Moses and of Jesus. I was
particularly interested in the way the image of God's compassion as a woman is traced through the Old Testament by
Phyllis Trible so that the great reversal of God may be seen in
the love story of the Song of Songs and in the story of
sisterhood between Ruth and Naomi.[28] I was also interested in
the way in which the image of Rachel weeping for the children
who were to be restored to her appears in Matt. 2:18. Herod
attempts to kill the Messiah by slaughtering the male children
in Bethlehem, and mothers are again left weeping.

Perhaps the most important aspect of the art of anticipation
is our own *actions* in living out the text. When we find ways to
live out the story of the text as part of our own story and share
this with others, the text yields many new insights. Jon
Sobrino, in his book *Christology at the Crossroads*, has
pointed out that the word of the Bible is not so much already
given fact, but something to be done.[29] The Gospels were not
written by professors, but by apostles. It is in apostleship,
joining in God's liberating mission, that the story of New
Creation in Jesus Christ comes to be known and understood.
We become partners in Christ's story and witnesses to the
hope of God's future when we live out that hope. The text may
be lived out in at least four different ways: living with the text
in our minds and hearts over a period of time; sharing the
stories of the lives of others in the group and especially those
of oppressed groups that illuminate the text; looking back at
the way our own stories might illuminate the text; and living
with it over the years in expectation that God might speak
through it to us in other circumstances.

It is difficult to describe the ways that we might live out the
texts in Jeremiah 31 which are so rich in the memory and
experience of the Hebrew and Christian communities. Also it
is difficult to discuss stories and actions when I am sharing
them with readers rather than with a community of persons
gathered together. When I first discussed these texts with
others it was in relation to a Bible study by the National

Meeting of Women for Leadership Development held at the United Church of Christ in Cincinnati. In and through the inspiration and hassle of the meeting God seemed to be making us new so that we might join in the business of New Creation. Representatives of Women's Fellowship groups and feminists of the Women's Task Forces found themselves united in one sisterhood that reversed the usual polarization between such groups. Other small reversals have already been noted. Each time I begin to reflect on the texts and discuss them with others new actions and stories come to light in the continuing spiral of action/reflection.

In the art of anticipation we never reach a conclusion, because the horizon of God's future moves ahead of us in many unexpected ways. The text is always understood provisionally in the light of confirmation from the other end of history that is yet to be fulfilled. Nevertheless we do gain insights and clues for new ways of critical and committed listening and action. These *clues* to what the text might be saying in the light of God's intended future can be tested in the light of tradition. Do they help to continue the action of God in handing over Christ into the hands of coming generations and nations? In what way do they challenge our social, economic, and religious traditions? How is Christ breaking into our lives now in concrete anticipations of God's intended future? In the discussion of Jeremiah the two clues most helpful to me in trying to image theology as anticipation were that we should expect the unexpected in thinking from the other end of New Creation and that the business of new creation involves a willingness to "go out of business."

The clues almost immediately lead us to look at the text again and to find new questions in the light of those new insights. In prophetic interpretation, there seems to be an overspill whenever the promise is fulfilled. That which is expected is changed by God's action and a new expectation is discovered in the very process of fulfillment. This certainly is what happened in the fulfillment of the covenant and its transformation through the experience of nationhood, exile, and restoration. The New Covenant in Jesus Christ both fulfilled and transformed the expectations of new covenant, so that we continue to look for "more to come." So too in the art of anticipation, there is no conclusion, only "more to come" as we provide space for one another to grow as partners in the action and reflection of theology.

The art of anticipation is not the only way to reflect seriously on the meaning of God's promise in our lives. Not only liberation theologians but also biblical scholars and educators are constantly at work in this area, trying to provide ways that our lives might come to be shaped by God's Word.[30] For instance, Leander Keck has written about steps in the renewal of preaching and Walter Wink about "dialectical hermeneutic" as a creative process of biblical study.[31] The history of the relationship of education and biblical studies over the last twenty years is well documented by Mary Boys in *Biblical Interpretation in Religious Education*, and Thomas Groome has developed a process of "present dialectical hermeneutics" as the interpretive method for his shared praxis approach to Christian religious education.[32] Groome's interpretation is similar to the art of anticipation in that it moves back and forth between our present action/reflection, the biblical story, and our shared vision. The art of anticipation is not particularly unique as a method. Rather, it is an attempt to spell out one way we might learn partnership in anticipating New Creation. Its particular agenda then is not so much the method, but the shared process of thinking from the other end.

THEOLOGICAL MINISTRY

Theological ministry of anticipation involves us in providing space where the overspill of insights can happen in a multiplication of partnership. I experienced this in October 1979 in leading a Bible study on Isa. 25:6-9 with professional theologians at the Commission on Faith and Order of the National Council of Churches. The passage images a time when all the peoples will gather on the holy mountain of the Lord to share in a feast of liberation and blessing. The theme of the meeting was "Jesus and the Poor," and the study was set in a time of worship and meditation so that we could reflect together not only on our own intellectual or critical questions but also on the questions of the poor whose stories were presented at the meeting: those from Latin-American *comunidades de base;* those laid off in the Mahoning Valley steel industry relocations; or those served by the Catholic Worker house in St. Louis. The question of the poor seemed clearly to be the question of justice. If this is God's intention, why is it that I do not have bread to eat? If this is God's intention, why does it make so little difference in the life of the church?

One of the small group of biblical scholars considered what women might see in the passage. They noticed that God is the one who prepares the meal and provides the hospitality, and that the image of full community and shalom is seen in the doing away with the veil of sorrow from all the nations (Isa. 25:7). It was also noted that women, whether poor or not, have been restricted from coming to the table of the Lord and from serving at that table. They therefore are also suspicious of any easy promises that *all* are intended to be present. The brief study did not solve any critical problems, but it was a moment in the meeting when persons could enter into the story of their faith and listen to what it was saying in the light of the agenda of the poor and marginalized. They also had an opportunity to share in a multiplication of insight as partners in theology. The Commission members also were invited to commit themselves to action that would point to the reality of God's justice in a service of anointing for justice.

In providing space where shared action and reflection on God's promise can take place, theological ministry joins with educational ministry and prophetic ministry as the style of partnership for service. These gifts of service make it possible for the witnessing and learning community to be a community of anticipation that thinks and acts from the other end.

Community of Anticipation

Theological discernment is a gift of the Spirit given to the community of faith so that it can continue equipping the saints for the work of ministry. Through this discernment people are able to serve one another in mutual theological ministry. This ministry shares in all the dimensions of faith: building confidence in God's love as a community of faith; building commitment to live out the story of God's liberating action as a community of freedom; and building knowledge of the story and its future promise through a community of anticipation. There are many ways that communities of faith have reflected on the meaning of God's future and interpreted it for their lives. Some of these are already seen in the various perspectives on New Creation in the New Testament. According to Elizabeth Fiorenza, the New Testament interprets the end of history as *already present* in the resurrection of Jesus Christ and also as *not yet present* until the return of Christ and the fulfillment of New Creation.[33] Both views are expressed in various overlapping ways with emphasis on the future fulfillment of God's promise in the writings of Paul, Mark, Matthew, Luke, and Revelation, and emphasis on the present reality of salvation in John, Ephesians, and other post-Pauline writings. The "already/not yet" character of God's action is expressed in all the writings, but there is a tendency to stress the present life of the church rather than the future transformation of all creation in the later writings. As the churches became a part of the established social structures of their society, they lost their sense of future expectancy and turned their eyes away from the prophetic message of justice among the nations. Instead, salvation was focused on the destiny of the individual soul. In a community of anticipation the various perspectives on future will be present as we speak of future as both individual and social salvation; as both present and still to be realized.[34] But it is important not to lose the balance between these aspects of the realization of God's promised future.

One important way of maintaining these elements in tension is to view our theological ministry as a means of discerning the newness of God's creation breaking into the present and impelling us to live out a new reality of partnership with others. All members of a community of anticipation are involved in the talk of theological ministry as they act and reflect on the meaning of the calling of Jesus Christ.[35] In this sense, everyone, no matter what the person's training or job, is called to be an *amateur theologian:* someone who does theology for the "love of it," in response to an amateur God who does things "for the love of us." Those who have a particular gift for discernment receive special training and may become professional theologians, but their work in the community continues to be for the love of the gospel and the community (I Cor. 9:23).

One possible way of training persons as animators who evoke the gifts of theological ministry among others is to train them as *worldly theologians*.[36] Such persons are not necessarily professional theologians and not necessarily clergypersons. They are people educated to do theologically and educationally whatever they do. Their theological education has the purpose of equipping them to interpret biblical and church traditions in a variety of worldly contexts, including church, business, arts, government, education, and family. Ideally such persons would have double competency. They would be able to earn a living as a nurse, teacher, lawyer, social worker, doctor, etc., while at the same time sharing their gifts of theological ministry with the communities needing this ministry for their particular mission in the world. Persons such as this are already present in many congregations and communities for social change as people enter seminary in a second-career choice or choose theological studies as a means of learning to reflect on their work in a variety of fields. For instance, Yale Divinity School has an increasing number of students who come to seminary after raising families or pursuing other lines of work. There are students in joint degree programs with education, law, medicine, social work, and organizational management. This style of worldly theologian would make possible a continuing theological ministry in churches and other sectors of society where clergy are not available or not wanted. As amateurs in theology, communities of anticipation would be able to look for resources in theological reflection among laity and among nonprofessional theologians and to develop a new style of partnership.

Going out of Business

The purpose of theological ministry is to go out of business, as knowledge of God is more and more internalized in the lives of those who participate together in theological reflection. If Jeremiah's image of new covenant implies a time when teachers are no longer needed, then going out of business may be a sign of this hoped-for future. Educators, pastors, prophets, and theologians do not need to fear such a style of ministry for two reasons. First, in the time before the fulfillment of New Creation there are always those who want to hear more of "the story of Jesus" that we love to tell. When some learn to tell it for themselves, we are set free to share the gospel with others. Secondly, many types of ministry or service are designed to go out of business. When persons, society, or the environment are restored to health, wholeness, or balance and no longer need to be served, this is a cause of rejoicing and a sign of freedom. What *does not* go out of business is partnership. People not needed in a particular form of ministry or service are still needed in the continuing celebration of Christ's koinonia creating presence. They are still joined with others in a common commitment to Jesus Christ and they continue as partners, ready to give a hand where one or the other is serving or being served.

Two of the clues for God's New Math of partnership, discussed in Chapter 1, are particularly helpful here in our discussion of going out of business. The *minus factor* in partnership relationships is a clue for theological ministry. For in this style of ministry there should be a large amount of calculated inefficiency in what we do. This is a form of service that allows space for others to act and reflect together and to learn out of that process to multiply their own gifts of theological reflection. Teaching different members of a congregation to lead worship and preach, for example, is best accomplished by using sufficient time and care so that others learn to do the tasks without coaching. The teaching role then becomes one of mutual encouragement as different persons learn to innovate and to go on with the tasks. This is a pattern of Jesus in his own teaching, according to the Gospel of John. In the last discourses John pictures Jesus commissioning his disciples, not as servants, but as friends who are to share in the task of ministry (John 15:15).

A second clue follows from the minus factor. Going out of business in theological ministry means that there is only *temporary inequality* among partners. The various gifts of the Spirit are distributed unequally, but the distribution is only provisional. The Spirit raises up new persons with new gifts for the mission of the church in the world and those who were knowledgeable in one matter are not necessarily so for the next task. Theological ministry assumes that the teaching and learning process will be one in which more and more persons are able to share their particular skills and knowledge. This often means that curriculum facilities and education programs in churches have to be of the do-it-yourself variety. The design has to fit the particular gifts and needs for growth in that particular group of people.

The extra time is often a form of calculated inefficiency, because shifts in design mean that more persons have physical and intellectual access to leadership roles. Those in wheel-chairs can move into the chancel or church school classrooms; those with less education can be important peer teachers in partnership development; those who have never been encouraged to use their hands can find the joy of sharing in simple projects with persons of many ages; those afraid of any form of social involvement can become involved through work in preparation for a community hearing or in caring for a particular refugee family. In one congregation the writing of a church school curriculum involved a few persons who were empowered to carry out the task and to "waste" a good deal of time designing the material for that congregation. Yet the result was that a much wider group of people were able to participate in the learning process because the program was designed to fit their particular gifts and needs, to speak to their context. Those who before could not teach because they could not use a printed curriculum suddenly found themselves able to join in a cooperative teaching project that made use of many skills. This was symbolized in the response of one teacher to an appeal for additional church school teachers. She exclaimed, "The lessons are so easy and so much fun, I don't see why anyone wouldn't want to do it!"[37]

Education for partnership takes place when we become partners together in small anticipations of New Creation. These anticipations happen in our lives as we act and think from the other end of history, looking for God's reversals of injustice, suffering, ignorance, and pain and joining in God's liberating actions. When this happens we are neither surprised nor fearful about going out of our usual business in order to be part of the business of God's New Creation. Theology of anticipation is not a new theology nor a new method. But it is a part of God's New Math. It hints at ways to live our lives out of the future as partners in God's liberating action. I have tried to demonstrate that this art of anticipation is both possible and helpful by designing each chapter in this book as a continuing process of questioning our actions and those of society in the light of the biblical message of New Creation. You might say the whole book is a "Going out of Business Sale" for those who want to join with others as partners in doing their own theology of anticipation.

5

PEDAGOGY FOR OPPRESSORS

Partnership education for members of oppressor groups includes a pedagogy that can assist them to see the world in a new perspective. By discovering new ways of relating to people and our environment we also discover new possibilities for ourselves and for those who find themselves at a disadvantage in society. Jim Hood, a member of my seminary class on Education for Partnership, writes of a small incident in his own life that illustrates the possibilities of such a discovery of solidarity. On a brief Thanksgiving visit to his family in Florida, Jim and his twelve-year-old brother, Alan, were swimming in the pool and trying to think of some kind of game to play together:

> At first I tried to devise a competition which involved working against the other person to get a ball to the opposite end of the pool. Alan didn't want to do anything like that and I surprised myself by not pushing for it. Instead, we worked together to create a noncompetitive game in which we both cooperated in trying to push the ball from one end to the other without picking it up. Our efforts were not at all contrived or forced—the game evolved naturally out of our cooperation—and not only was the experience fun as it occurred, but it also strengthened our friendship. . . . Both of us learned something: a new game *and* a way of being and working together. The experience was one of freedom in that it freed us both from traditional roles and that it opened us up toward new possibilities, new ways of cooperating.[1]

Such a shift in perspective is crucial for all who wish to become partners, for partnership requires learning to "sit where others sit" and to share their experiences. Yet many people have a veil before their eyes. They see suffering, oppression, and inequality in their own towns and cities, and across the world on the television screen, but they do not know that the myths of equal opportunity, individualism, personal and national pride cover over many of the ways that interlocking systems of racism, sexism, classism, and imperialism perpetuate this suffering in the name of freedom.

"Pedagogy for oppressors" is a play on the title of Paulo Freire's book *Pedagogy of the Oppressed.* In his book Freire contrasts pedagogy of liberation with that of domination and calls for a pedagogy forged with and for the oppressed in the struggle to regain their humanity. According to Freire, the oppressors cannot free themselves from a system that holds them and dehumanizes them even as they benefit from it. They need the oppressed to unveil the world of oppression and begin the process of transformation.[2]

If this is true, it would seem to me that the first stage of pedagogy in the United States should include a pedagogy *for* the oppressor as well as a pedagogy *of* the oppressed. Both formal and informal educational structures usually reinforce the values and interests of the dominant groups in a society. Therefore, in order to work toward liberation in which groups can become partners we need a pedagogy for oppressors designed to unveil injustice and social sin. Together with the oppressed, those who wish to move toward liberation can express their own need for help by asking the oppressed to assist them in a discovery of solidarity in groaning. The second stage in which oppression is put out of business and a new human being, neither oppressed nor oppressor, emerges would seem to be that of which Jesus speaks in Luke 4:19 as the "year of liberation."[3]

Those who wonder about the meaning of oppression do not have to look far in the Bible and in the ministry of Jesus to find it. Already in Luke's account of the beginning of Jesus' ministry we hear that he has come to "set at liberty those who are oppressed" (Luke 4:18; Isa. 58:6). Literally, they are the "crushed ones," the "bruised" of society; the nonpersons who have no "room to breathe" or to live as human beings.[4] They are the ones to pay for the freedom and privilege of oppressors. If persons and groups who benefit from the exploitation of others are going to be set free to share in the partnership of New Creation, they need to understand the meaning of God's liberating action for their own particular context.

WHO PAYS FOR FREEDOM?

In the summer of 1979, Krister Stendahl and I gave lectures at the Shalom Center, Augustana College, South Dakota. Here, in the heartland of the United States, a group of women and men seriously considered the theme of Christian Liberation: The Gift and Task. Most of us were white, middle-class, North American Christians. In a sense we were engaged in a pedagogy for oppressors, addressing questions of liberation to our own churches, society, and lives. Stendahl made a good beginning with that pedagogy by pointing out that *freedom costs* and it should be paid for by those who can afford it.[5] This is not the way payment is usually made. The United States needed free land and the Native Americans and Spanish Americans paid. We needed free markets and first the black slaves paid, and then the Third World countries paid as dumping grounds for our surplus. Whenever the dominant group in society moves to protect its privilege it is usually those who cannot afford to pay who are hit with increased taxes and decreased social service and jobs (II Sam. 12:1-7a).

The biblical view of New Creation asserts that liberation is an action of God's righteousness in which things are put right. It is God who pays for this "new birth of freedom."[6] As we saw in Chapter 1, Paul is emphatic in declaring,

> For our sake [God] made him to be sin who knew no sin, so that in him we might become the righteousness of God. (II Cor. 5:21)

God's righteousness is what we usually understand as justice or justification. It is the way in which God is faithful to the covenant promises of shalom for all creation by putting things right in the world and inviting us into a partnership of righteousness. This appeal to God's righteousness is a familiar theme of prophetic ministry, as we saw in the discussion of both Exodus 15 and Jeremiah 31. It is described over and over again as setting at liberty those who are oppressed, so that creation is mended (Isa. 58:1-9).

The prophetic word of comfort for the oppressed is also a word of judgment for the oppressor. Often we miss the "right word" when we identify with the wrong persons in the biblical story. This is very well illustrated in Luke's account of the beginning of Jesus' ministry in his hometown of Nazareth (Luke 4:16-30). Many of us are familiar with this passage as comforting words about Jesus' baptism and call to a ministry of service. We identify with Jesus in this ministry and seek to live out this life-style in our churches. Yet it is possible that the message might come home more sharply if we were to identify with the townspeople of Nazareth. When they saw that the message of freedom was not going to benefit them they sought to destroy the messenger. In quoting the words of Isa. 61:1–2, Jesus announces that the year of liberation has arrived. The poor no longer have to pay for the freedom of others, for God will set the people free, but those who reject this new reality will have to pay. The price of solidarity in the groaning of the oppressed is repentance and justice.

Year of Liberation
In ch. 4:16–19, Luke describes Jesus' call as a prophet and messiah-king who brings God's promised liberation. God's Spirit has been poured out upon him so that he can proclaim the good news of God's salvation to the poor, the people most in need of divine help. The signs that the time of liberation has already arrived in the ministry of Jesus are listed by making use of a quotation from the Greek version of Isa. 61:1–2a and Isa. 58:6.[7] It means healing, release of prisoners of war, recovery of sight, freedom for the oppressed, and the proclamation of God's jubilee of liberation.[8]

Matthew and Mark begin their description of the Galilean ministry of Jesus with a "capsule statement" of what Jesus began to preach.[9]

The time is fulfilled, and the kingdom of God is at hand; repent, and believe in the gospel. (Mark 1:15)

Luke, on the other hand, tells the story of Jesus' rejection at Nazareth that occurs later in Mark and Matthew (Mark 6:1–6; Matt. 13:54–58). In this way he dramatizes the message of liberation. Already the signs of the New Creation are present, signs that bring both blessing and judgment. In Luke's version of the Beatitudes this is underlined by a corresponding list of woes. The poor and oppressed, and those who share their lot as Jesus' disciples, can look forward to their needs being satisfied by God, and the rich and popular will suffer divine judgment (Luke 6:20–26).[10]

In the East Harlem Protestant Parish we used to recite these words of Jesus as our Parish Purpose at every service of worship. In a setting of poverty, racism, and oppression they were *good news*. Jesus had come to set the oppressed at liberty, and it was our task to carry out this ministry. As far as I can remember, no one ever paid much attention to the other side of the Year of Jubilee, or wondered why Luke dropped off the second half of verse 2 in Isaiah 61 which speaks of "the day of vengeance." Our agenda was clear. We sang, "This is the year of Jubilee; . . . My Lord has set [the] people free . . . " and tried as best we knew how to live out that freedom.[11] Yet the other side of the Jubilee tradition is there and it is important for those who are white, middle-class Americans to take a look at it. John Yoder describes the jubilee year as

> the time when the inequities accumulated through the years are to be crossed off and all God's people will begin again at the same point.[12]

The legislation of Lev. 25:1–34 makes provision both for a sabbath year of rest every seven years and for a jubilee year of liberation every fifty years in which everything that came from the Lord is returned so that it can be redistributed.

Even if the legislation was mainly "Zion's fiction," we know that there was at least some attempt to carry it out by King Zedekiah, who proclaimed liberty to all Hebrew slaves as part of a covenant renewal ceremony. The city of Jerusalem was under siege and the people hoped to win God's favor. However, the owners took back their slaves and the covenant was again broken.[13] In Jer. 34:17 we hear the words of condemnation spoken by the prophet:

> Therefore, thus says the LORD: You have not obeyed me by proclaiming liberty, every one to [their] brother and to [their]

neighbor; behold, I proclaim to you liberty to the sword, to pestilence, and to famine, says the LORD.

The prophetic vision of jubilee as both a year of liberation and a time of judgment came to be a description of God's future action of salvation. On the "Day of the Lord" God's righteousness and justice was to be fully established.[14] The words in the RSV translation of Luke 4:19 read, "the acceptable year of the Lord." They reflect this metaphor for God's future judgment and liberation and point to its present actualization in the ministry of Christ. The Hebrew text of Isa. 61:2a reads, "year of the LORD's favor." It may refer here to the release of the people from captivity, and it also reflects the jubilee description of the time God has appointed in order to bring about salvation.[15]

The cost of this new freedom of jubilee is clear, both in the prophetic tradition and in Jesus' call to ministry. The cost is that oppressors go out of business. God's freedom is not a freedom of equal opportunity, but a freedom of justice in community.[16] No one is to have the freedom to be master over others, because all Pharaohs are eliminated. No one is free to compete with the others to establish their individual rights. Rather, as Moltmann has pointed out, God's freedom is granted in community with others.[17] The jubilee is an opportunity for new exodus so that God's people can again form a new social community to match the vision of God's freedom. It is exodus spelled out in terms of social salvation.[18] To understand some of the ways that the new exodus happens in our lives we need to look at the second half of Luke's story of Jesus' rejection at Nazareth.

Solidarity in Groaning

When Jesus finished reading Isaiah he handed back the scroll, sat down, and began to preach (Luke 4:20–22). Regardless of what Jesus meant by the words, "Today this scripture has been fulfilled in your hearing," Luke wants to stress that these are the opening words of Jesus' public ministry. "Today" refers not only to fulfillment of the prophecy in Jesus' own ministry but also to its continuing fulfillment in the life of the Christian community (Luke

7:18–23). In contrast to Mark's account, in which the people are hostile from the beginning (Mark 6:1–3), Luke presents the people of Nazareth as responding favorably to Jesus' prophetic proclamation until they remember that this is only "Joseph's son" (Luke 4:22).

In the face of their growing doubt and hostility Jesus indicates that he will carry his ministry to the Gentiles if he is rejected by the Jews (Luke 4:23–27). Having heard Jesus preach, the people expect him to perform miracles and healings to confirm his message, but it appears that since his words were not met with faith, he cannot and will not perform signs. Jesus' words produce rage among his audience and they seek to kill him by throwing him off a cliff, or possibly by stoning him as a false prophet (vs. 28–30; Deut. 13:1–5; Luke 13:34–35). Jesus escapes, but the shadow of rejection and cross hangs over Jesus' ministry from the very beginning.[19]

Into this story Luke has already woven many of the motifs of his gospel message: prophetic word of promise; endowment by the Spirit; good news for the poor; the year of liberation; hostility of the Jews; and mission to the Gentiles.[20] Of particular interest to us here is the rejection of Jesus' message of God's solidarity with the oppressed. It is certainly not difficult to understand why the people were angry. Using modern terminology, we might say that Jesus confronted their classism in claiming that an ordinary townsperson could be the Messiah—God's chosen instrument of salvation. In Mark's account it is even possible that the people were calling him a "bastard" by saying that he was Mary's son (Mark 6:3). Jesus also confronted their racism in declaring that the jubilee would be for all people.

We are often offended when we perceive that the ordered reality of our lives is being challenged and disturbed. I remember a series of lectures that I gave to a large audience of predominantly white, male clergy at Princeton Seminary.[21] I could not understand the hostile reaction to my very moderate discussion of the meaning of God's call until I realized that the reaction was not just to my words, but to me. I was being perceived by some people as a threat because I was a female clergyperson and professional theologian. Simply by standing there I disturbed the status quo and confronted the structures of sexism so important to the self-identity of the male clerical structure of the church. The cost I paid in receiving hostile questions and in rejection of my message was very small. But the real cost of overcoming the structures of alienation in the world is great. The cost is one that neither I nor my audience wanted to pay. The cost is the willingness to leave the "fleshpots of Egypt" and begin the new exodus of social salvation (Ex. 16:3). Dorothee Soelle describes this cost in a poem about Israel's departure from Egypt, and the "good life" which came to an end. They had to decide whether they wanted

> the supermarkets of Egypt
> or the march through the desert
> forty years
> permanent revolution.[22]

To use modern terminology again, the cost of freedom with justice is reparations. It is working for the mending of creation by acting in response to the pain of others. Krister Stendahl has pointed out that the words of Jesus in Matt. 5:23–24 are often heard in the wrong way.[23] We hear that we need to be reconciled to our neighbor before offering our gift to God in worship. However, the text points out that "your brother has something against you." It is not just a matter of forgiving or asking forgiveness but rather a matter of reparations. Reconciliation takes place by acting to remove the cause of the offense. The oppressors are not being asked to feel guilty. As Stendahl says, "The poor can't eat guilt." They are being asked to act in such a way as to address the causes of injustice so that the poor can eat food.

This is the "predicament of the prosperous."[24] We want to be part of God's saving and liberating action but we don't want to give up the "fleshpots" provided by structures of racism, sexism, and classism and all the other forms of injustice. We reason that God's mercy and forgiveness and the fact that Christ has paid the cost of freedom and reconciliation should mean that there is "free grace." Grace may be free, but it is not "cheap grace." God shows mercy in paying reparations for the oppressed, those excluded from the benefits of the dominant society. God also shows mercy for oppressors by welcoming them as participants in the continuing process of putting things right. God's bias for outsiders, widows, strangers, orphans, the sick, handicapped, and the poor is the same bias shown in the exodus event. It is a bias toward justice. The captives receive liberty because that is what they need. The blind see and the lame walk for the same reason. The good news is that we are all invited to share in this affirmative action process by doing our particular part in the mending of groaning creation.

The good news for oppressor groups is that there is still time in God's patience for us to share both the groaning and the glorious liberty of creation (Rom. 8:21). God's mercy is our opportunity for imaginative and constructive repentance. Luke considers riches to be evil, but he repeats, along with Matthew and Mark, the saying that it is easier for a camel to go through the eye of a needle than for the rich to enter the Kingdom of God (Luke 18:25–27). The context indicates that the impossible idea of giving up one's riches is possible in God's New Creation. As Marie Augusta Neal puts it:

> The utopian society Jesus proclaims in which the rich will actually give up their goods, though impossible for human beings to achieve on their own, can be achieved with the help of God. That, I think, is the great hope of today.[25]

Freedom is the impossible possibility of God's New Creation already at work in our lives. But freedom does cost and everyone pays for the establishment of justice and the mending of creation. God in Christ has paid on the cross. The oppressed have paid and continue to pay more when they join the new exodus. The oppressors also pay in repentant action to restore the structures of freedom, justice, and a sustainable society. Jesus' sermon in Nazareth is a call to partnership in God's jubilee event. It is no small wonder that when we stood up to declare the Parish Purpose in East Harlem it was a part of the closing benediction of our worship service. As participants in the impossible possibility of God's jubilee we went forth to show and tell the good news to those whom the world says "have no possibility."

THEOLOGY FOR OPPRESSORS

Some people are sure to resent all this talk of oppressors and oppressed, but the fact is that there is no possibility of partnership with God, one another, and all creation unless we acknowledge that we are all caught in social sin. This is not to deny that there are personal actions of sin and injustice, but rather to emphasize that these actions are manifestations of the structures of sin and separation in our world. Systemic oppression arises from the interaction of various institutions and groups comprising a social system. It continues to function according to its particular set of rules and patterns unless the "rules of the game" are changed.

In the class on education for partnership a group of students decided to learn about the possibility of different perceptions of society and of social systems by having us play a stacked game of Monopoly in which people started out already rich or already broke. Some people tried to subvert the game and to form a socialist collective so that everyone would be welcome on Boardwalk at Atlantic City, but others refused to join the collective. As we reflected on the difficulty of systemic change, it came to us that if the rules of the game were changed so radically that all were welcome, there would not be a game anymore! The intent of God's New Creation is to end the old games of power and dominance. We may not be able to live up to this New Math, but God has given us the opportunity to work out our own liberation in fear and trembling (Phil. 2:12).[26]

This discussion of structures of oppression, domination, and injustice is not an attempt to reduce God's action to politics, but rather an invitation to share God's action in the political, social, and personal aspects of creation.[27] The invitation calls for the development of a theology for oppressors that seeks to name reality from the perspective of God's jubilee. Such theology has to begin where many of us find ourselves, among the fleshpots of the so-called First World.[28] In this specific context there is much that needs to be done in developing ways the oppressors and oppressed can become partners in education.

Theology Among the Fleshpots

One might say that most theology written in the context of the white, male church and university establishments of the First World is theology *of* oppressors, developed among the "fleshpots of Egypt." But what interests us here is the response that people are making to the challenge of Third and Fourth World people. How do theologians respond to challenges from racially and economically oppressed peoples? How do they include the voices of women in their searching out God's intention for mending creation? How can they develop a liberation theology *for* their own situation of enslavement? The response of North American white males has grown out of biblical studies on the meaning of God's liberating action and out of challenges to action and reflection that have come from theologians speaking from the Third World and from the perspective of blacks, women, Asians, Hispanics, and Native Americans. The effect of this in relation to biblical studies in the work of Krister Stendahl and Walter Brueggemann, to name only two persons, has been documented earlier in this chapter.

A similar effect in developing a dialogue around black and Latin-American liberation issues may be seen in Frederick Herzog's *Justice Church* and Robert McAfee Brown's *Theology in a New Key.* An increasing number of books are being published by white, male theologians which incorporate insights and issues from liberation theologies into the framework of systematic theology. Examples of this would be Peter Hodgson's *New Birth of Freedom* and Daniel Migliore's *Called to Freedom.*[29] This dialogue and attempt to forge a theology for oppressors has been aided by a Working Group on Liberation Theology, chaired by Douglas Meeks and Clarke Chapman, which has been meeting since 1976 as part of the American Academy of Religion and the Society of Biblical Literature. This dialogue has also been on the agenda of many of the participants in the project groups of Theology in the Americas.[30]

White, middle-class women play a special part in the developing of theology among the fleshpots. They are members of both groups: those who prepare the meat for the pots and those who have meat to eat. Because they, like

Moses, are status inconsistent as members of a subordinate group who share benefits of the dominant group, they may also have some of the zeal of Moses in working to eliminate this divided situation. Not only do they identify with both situations from the inside but also they carry with them the ambiguity we all feel in finding ourselves in situations where we are oppressed and yet are also oppressing others. Both Marie Augusta Neal and Dorothee Soelle have been mentioned earlier in this chapter in reference to Neal's interest in *theology of relinquishment* of First World affluence and Soelle's interest in *theology of resistance* to the prevailing social trends of Western society.[31] This is also my own situation and interest and is one of the causes for my working out of both sides of oppression to develop *theology of partnership* for those who want to begin living out God's freedom now.

The European male theologian most involved in furthering this development of theology for oppressors is Jürgen Moltmann. With Douglas Meeks he published an article entitled "The Liberation of Oppressors" which seems to me to represent a careful attempt to spell out the two sides of oppression in their theological context. "Oppression destroys humanity on both sides, but in different ways: on the one side through evil, on the other side through suffering."[32] Although, as Freire has pointed out, the process of liberation must go on at the same time on both sides, faithfulness expressed out of suffering and out of evil is different, and liberation theologies need to address the different situations. Moltmann tries to move beyond the guilt and anger of oppressors by analyzing the way the structures of racism, sexism, and capitalism perpetuate evil. In each case these ideologies for the domination of one group by another result in the perpetuation of two forms of evil: the inner evil of self-justification and pride through myths of inferiority, and the outer evil of aggression and subjugation of other persons. Speaking of racism, Moltmann says that

> racism as self-justification and self-assertion manifests a super-human pride and in fact is nothing other than an inhuman anxiety. Those who identify being human with being white

destroy *themselves.* And because they always transpose their anxiety into aggression against others, they destroy community.[33]

He also points out that in racism and sexism one's own race and sex are misused as the basis of self-valuing and self-justification. In capitalism, however, it is the capital accumulated in smaller part by one's own labor and in larger part by the labor of many others that is misused as a source of unlimited accumulation of power. Every human being is doubly exploited, first by being identified as work power rather than as person, and second by being made slave to consumption in order to increase profit.[34]

The root cause of these structures of aggression and self-justification is named by Moltmann as love that is distorted. Love of God has become self-love in the form of hunger for power and will to subjugate. The possibility of change comes through the transformation of the human beings' relationship to God, to others, and to creation. The cost of this liberation is seen in God's suffering solidarity with the oppressed. Those who through faith seek this new relationship of freedom in community with others also pay the cost of refusing to conform to the status quo of this world (Rom. 12:2).

> Whoever wants genuine communion with the victims must become the enemy of their enemies. Thus if he or she comes from the ranks of the enemy, he or she will become a betrayer. To become free from the oppressive prison of one's society means to become a "stranger among one's own people."[35]

Partners in Power

In developing liberation theology with oppressor groups Moltmann and others make it clear that one of the major issues is our understanding of the distribution of power in the structures of society. Charles Brown has pointed to this as a key area in social ethics, suggesting that we should view power as a basic aspect of human life that promotes either "bonding" or "bondage." When power is expressed in relational terms it is "reciprocal, community-building and accountable" and promotes bonding between and among persons. When power is expressed in terms of domination and force it becomes "alienating and irresponsible" and gives rise to bondage.[36] Alternatives to *power as domination* need to be worked out so that people can grasp the possibility of *power as partnership*.

All too often people discover their dominant or subordinate position and take steps with others to change it without clearly recognizing the underlying ideology of power that is functioning to prevent the redistribution of power. Thus, for example, women and blacks work to gain access to the corporate or institutional pyramid of power without recognizing that the capitalist pyramid itself is dehumanizing. The oppressors' view of power needs to be contrasted to an alternative view if we are to find our way among the fleshpots of the First World. This view and one alternative can be illustrated in Betty Lehan Harragan's book, *Games Mother Never Taught You: Corporate Gamesmanship for Women,*[37] and Jean Baker Miller's book, *Toward a New Psychology of Women.*

Harragan views the business world as a game. The purpose of the game is to win. She analyzes the business game and language in its jargon of "military metaphor and sports vernacular" in terms that sound very much like U.S. foreign policy.[38] Power equals domination or mastery, or what Brown calls "bondage." There is no attempt to challenge the rules of the game so that everyone can play the game. In fact, Harragan claims that the corporate game is just like recreational games, "the meeting of *equals*"! The book documents in popular fashion how the game is played most of the time in the church as well as in the corporate and political world. By providing scorecards and a list of moves and players, it encourages us to see our world as a game that is *fun to play*.[39] This helps us see what some of the fleshpots look like, and it may even help women and others who have handicaps to distance themselves from the seriousness of the fray, but it also sets up all those who are not up to winning, so that they blame the victim (themselves) when the game is *no fun* at all.

But power does not necessarily need to be exercised in a continuing war game of divide and conquer. It can also be exercised responsibly as "bonding." This alternative is described by Miller. She contrasts power as ability to advance oneself and to control and destroy the power of others, with power as "capacity to implement" in ways that foster the human development of oneself and others.[40] While men are members of a group that believes it needs subordinates and views power as necessary for maintaining their self-image, women are members of a subordinate group and generally fear power and success in corporate or any other "gamesmanship." This fear is well founded, because women's independent exercise of power is generally met with rebuke from men who accuse them of being "uppity" or destructive, and of depriving or hurting others. According to Miller, valuable qualities more apparent in women's cultural and psychological roles, such as helping in the development of others, will not get them to the top at General Motors; in fact,

the characteristics most highly developed in women and most essential to human beings are *the* very characteristics that are specifically dysfunctional for success in the world as it is. . . . The acquisition of real power is not antithetical to these valuable characteristics. It is necessary for their full and undistorted unfolding.[41]

In the struggle to do theology among the fleshpots we must address ourselves to the way we exercise power as oppressors and oppressed. As Harragan and Miller illustrate, there are many ways to approach this question, but the different perspectives may help force us to a new partnership of thought and action. Certainly, alternatives are also being developed by men as well as women, but the example out of women's lives is particularly illuminating to our discussion because it springs out of the position of status inconsistency and thus speaks from both sides. One shorthand way of describing what we are about in working on theology and pedagogy for oppressors is to say that our goal is a solidarity of groaning with the oppressed on the part of the oppressors so that together as Christians we all become *status inconsistent,* claimed to live as God's partners, while still dwelling among those who play by the rules of old creation.[42]

CURRICULUM OF SUBVERSION

Who would choose to be status inconsistent rather than simply "on top"? Who would want to participate in a jubilee celebration based on personal and social loss of wealth and power? Such altruism is almost impossible for persons, let alone groups. Yet God's action of deliverance makes it possible for persons and groups to be freed from inhuman self-love and to be joined in community with those whom God is delivering from suffering. And there are members of the oppressor group who do work and pray for this possibility. Three books are illustrative of a variety of approaches to this mutual process of consciousness-raising and challenging to new action:

Straight/White/Male, edited by Glenn Bucher, is an invitation to persons like Bucher to risk liberation with him.[43] He describes his own story of socialization as a straight, white male in the United States and then contrasts this with the story of his conscientization. The book includes stories and perceptions of those who speak out of the black, female, and gay experiences as well as a discussion of the straight, white, male problem by members of the "club."

Servant Leadership: A Journey Into the Nature of Legitimate Power and Greatness, by Robert Greenleaf, develops the issues of partnership and power from the perspective of the elites of business and voluntary organizations. Out of a lifetime of work in areas of training and organizational management, Greenleaf focuses his analysis and educational advice in the area of leadership development for individuals and organizations. His contention is that the most important quality of leadership is that of service.[44] Only as elites begin to be motivated by this basic commitment to others in society will organizational renewal be possible.

Thomas Groome has developed the most elaborate form of pedagogy for the oppressor in his book *Christian Religious Education: Sharing Our Story and Vision.* His "Shared Praxis Approach" is a group process of dialogue in which Christians move together to name their present action, and to reflect critically on their own story and vision, in the light of the Christian Community Story and Vision.[45] This is then interpreted in the dialectic between the story and vision of the participants and the Christian Community Story and Vision. The approach, with specific guidelines for these five movements of action/reflection, is developed for use with all ages in structured educational settings. It reflects the response of a white, male clergyperson to the need for participatory education for liberation in the church.

All three of these books reflect the perspective that change is possible and that changes of consciousness and action will benefit the dominant group as well as those presently in subordinate positions. This is an important approach because groups are not likely to move against their present position of advantage unless forced to do so by pressure from below, or convinced to do so by peers on the basis of self-interest. In a sense, both things are happening today. Oppressed groups worldwide are challenging the dehumanizing actions of oppressor groups. At the same time there are those among the dominant groups that catch a vision of the possibility of a more human identity for all and move to advocate this change. In this setting God continues to call the church to become a sign of this impossible possibility of jubilee.

In discussing partnership consciousness in Chapter 2, I pointed out that a *curriculum of subversion* is most effective as a process of mutual learning among those who are searching for new identity. Theology and pedagogy for the oppressors are part of that search into our own identity and the way that history, culture, and personal life have been both oppressive and liberating. It takes place with oppressed groups who share their different perceptions of reality and of the gospel message so that the Word of God's liberating actions is heard in new ways. The curriculum of subversion is an intentional educational component of education for partnership *among those who have been sufficiently challenged by the vision of New Creation that their hearts and minds are at least in some small way open to new forms of personal and social partnership*. It is certainly not the only way of learning to participate in God's jubilee of liberation, but it provides a few clues to how we might learn to share in letting "the oppressed go free" (Isa. 58:6).

This particular curriculum of subversion may not look much like a "curriculum." I am using the word intentionally to refer to people's actions rather than to lesson plans or texts, because it is people and the actions of people that are the key medium of any message. People are the mentors of those who would learn, the source of ideas, the inspiration and support, and the new role models. It is people who interact in personal, social, and political settings who challenge and subvert our view of reality so that we may come to see and act differently.

I use the word "subversion" in the sense of undercutting our false consciousness of present reality so that we may participate in the reality of God's New Creation breaking into our lives. In this sense the clues point to ways God's Spirit might work among us to bring about our conversion in Christ as new human beings. The word itself was suggested to me by the book on educational reform entitled *Teaching as a Subversive Activity,* by Neil Postman and Charles Weingartner.[46] But the content of the curriculum was suggested to me by my own work as a teacher in church and seminary. Most of the work I do is pedagogy for the oppressor that takes place in largely white, middle-class structures in the First World. As a status-inconsistent theologian, I am constantly struggling with how to name reality for both oppressed and oppressor groups in such a way that we may hear God's invitation to partnership in groaning creation. The curriculum of subversion does not make any pretense at answering that question in any definitive way, but it does underline the need for many liberating pedagogies that spring out of the concrete situation of those who live in North America as members of oppressor groups.[47] In this particular context we need to explore ways we can become *free from* oppression in order to become *free for* partnership. In discussing the six clues for action in the curriculum, I will use a class at Yale Divinity School on Issues in Liberation Theology as one example of pedagogy for oppressors in theological seminaries.

Freedom from Oppression

Luke 4 presents the ministry of Jesus as part of God's year of liberation. Already God has begun to carry out this year and oppressed and oppressors alike are invited to become partners in making all creation new. As oppressors we are set free from our need for self-justification, because God pays for our freedom even while we are yet sinners (Rom. 5:8). We are also set free from the need to dominate others, because in Christ's death God shows us the cost of betrayal of our brothers and sisters. As we seek to be set free from our role in oppressive structures of society we need partners who help subvert us into being partners by acting out the impossible possibility of freedom from oppression. In this mutual process of subversion we need to learn to think from the other end, act for social change, and learn to be critical.

Thinking from the other end is not only a key aspect of the art of anticipation as we discussed it in Chapter 4. It is also a key for those who want to open their lives to the calling of God's Spirit. White, Western, male theology has often specialized in spelling out where we have come from in doctrinal statements that seek to describe and explain reality. To free ourselves to be open to God's promise we also need to speak clearly in hope statements that seek to contradict reality in the light of the future.[48] Descriptive thinking is often a trap for those who want to change the established patterns of society. This was brought home to me in the early 1960's when I attended a retreat of the Presbytery of New York City. There was nothing but talk about the way *these* churches and *that* city were decaying. I was so upset about this use of nostalgia as an excuse for inaction that I joined with a small group to write a booklet called *The City—God's Gift to the Church,* reminding persons that God loves the people of the city and has plans for its "future and hope" (Jer. 29:11).[49]

Openness to the unexpectedness of God's new reality comes from learning to turn things around so that we ask what we want to be free for and not just what we want to be free from. The life-style of Jesus of Nazareth is helpful in learning to live and think from the other end. Because of his vision of God's jubilee of liberation he was able to identify in the present with all the marginal persons in society and to include them in all the actions of his life. For example, even though he was a male, he was able to identify with women and treat them as the whole persons God intended them to become.

As we saw in the discussion of faith development, thinking from the other end can best be learned from persons who are only one step more developed in their ability to think in this way. Therefore, it is often peers whose thinking is only slightly more prophetic who are most able to communicate a new style of thinking. One way we practiced thinking from the other end in an elective class of about thirty women and men at Yale Divinity School was by working collectively to interpret a Bible passage using the *art of anticipation* described in Chapter 4. The passage, Matt. 5:27–28, was assigned to me for a Lenten preaching series at Yale. This "Hard Word About Adultery" led us to ask, not just what it means for men to lust in their heart, but also how this feels for women, and how Jesus' words point toward God's intention for a New Creation in which grace and not biology is our destiny.

Acting for social change is essential to any subversion of our understanding of the reality of structures of oppression as members of a dominant group. Behavior and attitudes are more likely to change if we have an opportunity to try out new ways of working for the rights of others. Those who are searching for their identity as Christians and as members of a particular culture and group need opportunities to try out their new perceptions. Churches, for instance, can provide valuable opportunities for trying out one's commitment to Christ and neighbor by involving a pluralistic group of persons together in projects such as those related to hunger, urban renewal, or energy. In one church they included participatory events for adults and youth in their retreat schedule. One retreat was a meeting with others in a planning conference seeking to structure a community development corporation related to the transportation needs in the city. Another time they went by bus to share in the packing of clothes for Church World Service at its center in Maryland.[50] Activities that provide a wide variety of experiences are important in the development of critical consciousness and testing out commitment.

Living out the life-style of Jesus in our lives involves acting out that story as partners with others so that we can learn what it means. In the class on Issues in Liberation Theology, I encouraged the members to relate other parts of their daily lives to the problems being discussed in black, Latin-American, and feminist theology. There was time in class to share notes about activities and to encourage members of the class to participate both individually and as a group in special lectures, demonstrations, petition writing, and worship services that helped to lift up Third World and feminist issues.

A closely related clue in the curriculum of subversion is *learning to think critically*. Opportunities for action should be designed to open up as much exposure as possible to situations of oppression and need. This provides a basis for action/reflection as a way of doing theology and it sometimes promotes cognitive dissonance. As Kohlberg has pointed out, it is the conflict between what is experienced and the former interpretation of that experience that leads us to develop new and more mature forms of interpretation. In order to challenge the culture of the oppressors in a critical way it is necessary to experience the results of that culture among those who must pay for it. For most people this direct exposure to "culture shock" in a different culture or subculture causes new awareness of self-identity and testing of prejudices. One of the best ways to discover what poverty is about is to test out socioeconomic theories by living in poverty in an urban or rural ghetto or a Third World country. Glenn Bucher gives a graphic illustration of this conscientization process for a straight, white male by describing his experience of culture shock in going to live in a black ghetto and teaching in a black college. A preferred experience would be to live in an alien situation, not as the one in charge, but as one who shares life and problems and learns critical awareness from inside the problem.[51]

Such exposure to different situations is a "teachable moment" for those who are open to being taught in partnership with others. A clue to changing attitudes of racism, classism, sexism, heterosexism, handicapism, and many other "isms" is that critical thinking about these issues grows out of sharing in solidarity with persons who are paying for the benefits of others. In the seminary class at Yale it was difficult to encourage such critical exposure except to support and nurture these ideas in the face of the dominant academic hierarchical point of view. I encouraged all persons to share their own socioeconomic and religious stories and how these shaped their understanding of identity in Christ and the meaning of salvation. Of particular importance was recognition of the diversity of stories and ideologies and their interaction with faith perspectives. The persons in the class who had extensive experience living, working, or studying in other cultures or subcultures provided a ferment of critical perspective for these discussions. Insofar as the class itself represented a different style and cultural perspective from the status quo of the school it promoted cognitive dissonance and critical thinking.

Freedom for Partnership

Our liberation from oppression is a long journey that involves us in a solidarity of groaning from the very beginning. Just as Jesus was despised and rejected because he identified with the reality of God's justice, those who share this identity will pay a price for being out of step with the world. Freedom for partnership is a gift from God that is discovered all along the way, in the midst of a common struggle to raise up signs of New Creation. It is nurtured by partners who know the cost of discipleship, yet welcome the chance to share and tell the love that transforms our lives. Three clues for subverting oppressors into living out their freedom to become partners are to think from the other side, love the questions, and identify with the marginalized.

Thinking from the other side is an important clue for learning partnership by being partners. We do not cease to belong to the oppressor group when we begin to understand reality from the perspective of the oppressed, but may discover one of the ways God opens the eyes of the blind. When our eyes are opened we begin to see things in a new perspective and we discover that perspectives on the world are never completely scientific or objective. For instance, from the "underside" things such as statistical studies, plans for development, or human rights platforms are not just matters of opinion, but are matters of life. Speaking out on human rights in Korea or the Philippines is not an academic matter. Nor is protesting the "disappearance of persons" in the hands of police in Argentina, or watching the floods destroy your crops in Bangladesh.

An important way of learning to think from the other side is to transfer one's own experience of victimization and alienation to that of the experience of others. Many persons have been able to understand something of the experience and questions raised by women because they have already been involved in the continuing and difficult struggle with white racism. Other people identify in their own way. Virginia Mollenkott, for example, tells us in her book, *Speech, Silence, Action!* that her basic identification with the other side was out of her own problem of obesity.[52] She has experienced continual prejudice and hurt because of her appearance in spite of the fact that it is due to a physiological problem that cannot be cured. Thus she is well aware of what it means to be marginalized and considered inferior because of a particular biological characteristic.

In the process of conscientization the "joke phase" is very cruel for the oppressed. Perhaps it can't be eliminated, but it can be avoided by learning to respect all people. In the Liberation Theology class, I tried to model this clue by thinking from the other side of the students. Rather than perpetuating an academic atmosphere of competition, domination, and dependence, I sought to build up cooperation in learning by respecting the contribution that each member had to make to the class. In offering to eliminate grades as a basis of evaluation I urged people to do quality research and reflection in order to share in the work with others, and to value one another's contribution to our theological process rather than to compete with one another in a form of "knowledge capitalism."

Loving the questions is another clue for the curriculum of subversion, for it is the questions and the people who dare to ask them that lead us toward new insights and discoveries. Breakthroughs in learning are dependent on experiment, questions, and even mistakes that can lead to new and unexpected insights.[53] Often people in oppressor groups turn away from questions because they feel insecure when they are supposed to know the answers. But we are most able to deal with our own fears and inadequacies if we recognize that questions are important whether or not we can answer them. An atmosphere in which no one is expected to know all the answers can help to undercut the liberal expert attitude.

In the class on theology I tried to be a partner in the learning process by admitting my own vulnerability and saying that I didn't know the answer to a particular question even when it might make me look stupid in the perspective of highly trained academic students. I also took the class members' questions seriously by beginning lectures on Christ, God, and salvation with insights and questions from their papers. They wrote reflection papers at the beginning of each section rather than at the end! Sometimes I would design the lecture in modules so that I could change its contents according to the questions of the students. In trying to develop a curriculum of subversion, loving the questions is important for everyone. In this type of curriculum we are questioning ourselves and our reality in the light of God's reality and our neighbor's need.[54]

Identifying with the marginalized means learning to sit where others sit. This does not mean that we can remove our race, sex, or personal, economic, and cultural history, but that it is possible to discover solidarity with others when we are willing to share in their own problems and situations. Usually this identification takes place around a common agenda or "third thing." In this way we are able to be partners because all persons bring a common commitment to the goal. When I lived and worked in East Harlem I shared the life and agenda of the church and the community and I identified with the marginality of that racial and economic ghetto, but I was still a white, educated person who could move out any time. My identification was part of a continuing struggle and commitment made over and over as a "betrayer of the betrayers."

Such identification is important in the face of false liberal consciousness that often turns into anger and backlash when the other group does not follow the liberal expert advice. In the class at Yale it was possible to promote this only in a very modest way by providing as much opportunity as possible for people from different marginal groups to present their own story, and for everyone to join in work groups and presentations related to sharing perceptions on such concerns as violence, homosexuality, racism, sexist language, human rights, and hunger. Fortunately for us there were enough women and Third World people in the class so that the stories and insights of the marginal groups were never marginal to the discussion of liberation theology.

What do we learn from these clues about thinking, acting, learning, loving, and identifying our way into solidarity with the oppressed? Perhaps most importantly that a pedagogy for the oppressor is needed. There is much work to be done in exploring possible educational, theological, psychological, sociological, and political resources for this task. In working on our own curriculums of subversion in church, school, and society, we need to give special attention to the way persons develop consciousness of partnership at points of *crisis* or transition in their lives. Ways of providing opportunity for *action* in situations that challenge persons to new thought and behavior need to be developed. In addition, the ways in which people *transfer* one experience of oppression to other situations would need to be explored carefully. Lastly, the identification of *significant persons* capable of stimulating growth in others by example, caring, and challenge is crucial to the development of a pedagogy for the oppressor. Clues to action in a curriculum of subversion are no substitute for working out our own liberation in fear and trembling. But perhaps for those who are searching for an authentic identity that is not oppressive to others the clues can assist in the development of consciousness so that people discover themselves on the road toward mutuality and partnership.

Partnership itself is a subversive activity because it is a new focus of relationship in Jesus Christ that sets us free for others. God has established this partnership with us and with all of groaning creation. In the midst of this world, God is subverting us into becoming partners in the struggle against oppression. Paul has described the longing to be free from oppression as a groaning of the whole creation in the pain of childbirth. Those who can identify with this pain may themselves become part of God's new birth of freedom.

> As we all know, up to the present time, the creation in all its parts groans with pain like the pain of childbirth. But not just creation alone groans; we ourselves, although we have tasted already the *aperitif* of the Spirit, we groan inwardly because we are still anticipating our adoption as children and the full liberation of our human existence. (Rom. 8:22–23)[55]

6

SPIRITUALITY OF LIBERATION

Education for partnership happens the same way with members of both oppressor and oppressed groups. We educate for partnership by being partners together in God's liberating action and by growing in our ability to anticipate New Creation through discovery and building of solidarity in groaning. Yet this process begins in different contexts and is developed in response to different questions. Solidarity in groaning for those who benefit from the oppression of others begins by developing a critical awareness and conscience about the reality of the situation. The question asked by those who seek to be open to God's liberating Spirit is how to work with others to relinquish the privileges that come from structures of domination. In the situation of oppression there is no need to discover what this reality looks like. Even those who are unable to name the reality of their situation still must struggle with it daily. The question they ask is how God's Spirit empowers them to actualize the freedom of New Creation. In the very long march through the wilderness, they want to learn how to "keep on keepin' on."

The experience of God's Spirit in our lives is very much an experience of the impossible possibility that we are set free to "keep on keepin' on" in the service of God and our neighbor. Like Jesus in Luke 4:18-19 we are anointed to preach good news and to proclaim the time of God's liberation (I John 2:20). The gift of the Spirit is a gift of liberation to become partners with others in God's liberating action. Because that Spirit breaks into our lives in the many unexpected ways of God's New Creation, it is often experienced as an interference

135

in our daily lives. Yet it is this very interference that reorients our lives, deepening and centering them in Christ, and opening them out toward others. One way of describing this spirituality of liberation is to speak of it as *the way God interferes in our lives* so that we may become partners in New Creation.

Spirituality is the way all Christians practice the presence of God's Spirit in their lives. In every age and situation Christians must examine the way they respond to God's call by remaining open to God's love and open to the needs of others. This spirituality often flowers in the midst of adversity, for it is there that the cost of freedom is discovered. The entire community of faith is nourished in its faith by this witness. The circumstances of our own times are no different. Even those who seek false spirituality by practicing inward comfort and shutting out the needs of the world are still challenged and discomforted by the witness of those whose spirituality leads them to share in resisting affliction even to the point of martyrdom.

In the United States the depth of black suffering is seen in the disturbing profundity of black spirituality. A powerful spirituality of liberation sustains the black community through preaching, prayer, and music.[1] The witness of martyrs like Martin Luther King is the seed of strength in the continuing struggle for freedom. The same thing is true in Latin America, where people live out the search for Christian spirituality in the new conditions of the church in the Third World.[2] In the midst of struggles against the oppression of the poor by the rich in their own countries and in the countries of the First World, the Spirit is at work bringing to light new and profound understandings of the biblical message in the context of sociopolitical oppression. Among women also a new spirituality of liberation is being born out of the collective search for ways that sexism can be eliminated and life can become more truly human for all.[3] In each case the spirituality is nurtured in a new context and expresses the presence of God in the lives of those who seek to build solidarity in that place.

In South Korea women relatives of political prisoners have experienced an outpouring of God's Spirit in their work for justice. Through political demonstrations, imprisonments, petitions, songs, and victory shawls, and through sheer courage in the face of an oppressive government, they have continued to witness to the innocence of their fathers, husbands, sons, and friends, and to call for restoration of human rights and democracy. Through ecumenical organizations the women have reached out to their sisters and brothers around the globe to advocate the cause of victims of oppression. Oo Chung Lee, president of Church Women United in South Korea, tells us that they began their struggles as traditional Korean women, unaccustomed to acting or thinking for themselves. But they soon learned to be full partners in the human rights movement, and found new opportunities for partnership with their men who returned home from jail. In working for justice, the women found liberation for themselves as well, a spiritual liberation that knows deep down that no matter what may happen "dark can't put out the light."[4]

CALLED TO BE PARTNER

Perhaps the story of the Gerasene demoniac seems like a strange story to use for discussing spirituality of liberation, but the events draw us right into the center of life before the Lord and with others. Here is a life in which God interferes to bring deliverance so that the man called Legion finds a new focus of relationship for his life and begins a new history with his people as a witness to the way Christ has set him free. This story is found in Mark 5:1-20 as part of a collection of miracle stories (Matt. 8:28-34; Luke 8:26-39). We are accustomed to approaching the story from the perspective of the nonbeliever. Therefore we focus on the issue of whether the miracle actually happened or why the swine were destroyed.[5] What if we approach the story from the perspective of the nonperson, someone, for instance, who is isolated outside the mainstream of society because he or she is old, sick, or poor? Our focus is then on how Christ can be present with them to deliver them.

In this light the miracle story is seen as an account of God's action of liberation very similar in form to that of the story of the call of Moses that was discussed in Chapter 3 (Ex. 3:1-4:17). In both stories the divine action of deliverance has already begun before the calling to partnership (Mark 5:1-8). The call is in the form of questioning and being questioned (vs. 7, 9). The dramatic sign that confirms God's call is not a burning bush as in the exodus story, but rather the drowning of the swine (vs. 11-13) and the cure of the man (vs. 14-17). The story concludes by sending the man to represent the Lord with his people. Just as Moses became God's prophet, Legion becomes an evangelist (vs. 18-20).

New Focus of Relationship

The story begins on the far side of the Sea of Galilee, perhaps in the vicinity of Gerasa, one of the Greek towns of the Decapolis. Here Jesus encounters "Everyone," a man so full of different personalities that he is called "Legion" (a regiment of soldiers numbering as many as 6,000).[6] He is one who in all his wild misery is a "riot of persons." In the wild, mad world of today it is easy to identify with this outcast. Often we too feel torn apart and full of fear, yet at the same time, longing for the possibility of freedom to be ourselves with others. Those of us, however, who are not marginalized in society should also practice identifying with those responsible for consigning the man to living death among the tombs. The message that Jesus proclaimed and embodied was that God's Kingdom was open to all persons regardless of their disability. We can hear again in this story the prophetic call to repent and live in covenant relationship with God. In the covenant the dangerous memory of slavery and deliverance was to transform society so that special care was taken for widows, orphans, strangers, and all the powerless ones in need of help (Ps. 146).

An obvious example of the need to act to eliminate such marginalization in our own society is the isolation of the handicapped, the mentally and physically ill, and the elderly. These people often are institutionalized in situations not dissimilar from the tombs, and in areas that are cut off and inaccessible to families and friends. This manner of punishing those who are different or in the way has its expected result in dehumanizing the people and aggravating their difficulties.

While we know that working with people in the context of their own communities and mainstreaming them in society is far healthier for them and for our own perceptions of reality, we find that things such as arms appropriations are more important than funds that would go for such social programs that would enable people to care for themselves together with others.[7]

In the story of the Gerasene demoniac the message that God welcomes the outsiders as partners in New Creation is acted out. The man is doubly outcast, not qualified even for Gentile society and certainly not qualified for Jesus' healing ministry among the Jews. Yet Jesus sees his need and welcomes him. He frees him from the demonic powers that chain him, and provides a new center and purpose for life. This new focus of relationship in his life is what frees the man from the riot of conflicting powers and makes it possible for him to come back into the center of society as a partner with others. Such an event is good news to all who find themselves enslaved by the structures of evil in their lives and in the structures of society.

The story is told very dramatically in four scenes and it is great fun to act it out. In East Harlem we enjoyed presenting it with the children. Ferocious paper bag masks were used for the demons and the swine, and great lengths of paper chain for Legion. Some sort of boat that Jesus could ride in was helpful, but the most important was something for the children to jump from as they portrayed the end of the pigs. One day during a hilarious rendition of these events a minister from out of town came to visit the program. He had to leave early, so I didn't talk with him afterward. About a year later I met him at a pastors seminar and he told me that he had enjoyed the creative program, but that he had been disappointed in our theology which allowed us to teach the children such a ridiculous story. I think in his critical awareness of the way miracle stories get inflated, he missed the good news that we were hearing as nonpersons, that God reaches out to set the prisoners free, that the chains of sickness, racism, and poverty can be broken by those who find a new focus of relationship in Christ. The clue we heard in East Harlem was that our identity was not just assigned by the dominant society. Rather, who we were was related to the mystery of God deciding to be with us as Liberator at the center of all our relationships.

Beginning of a New History

Verses 7-9 in Mark 5 include a rather awkward flashback that seems to indicate that Jesus has unexpectedly taken initiative and begun to cure this man called "Riot." The man runs and throws himself before Jesus, shouting in a loud voice, "What is *this thing* between you and me?" Jesus responds by asking the man's name. As we saw in the discussion of Exodus 3, knowing a person's name was understood as a way of gaining power over that person. But here there is no indication that Jesus uses the name to cure the man.[8] Rather, we seem to have a characteristic biblical pattern of God's address. In many stories, persons like Moses and Legion ask God or Christ to justify or prove themselves. In these cases the original question is usually answered by another question addressed to the questioner. In the encounter it is God who addresses us and asks our name, giving us a new identity and task (Isa. 43:1-3). The promise of God is identification with us in the midst of groaning toward liberation.

In a discussion of this text in the setting of a group of persons in training to be chaplains in hospitals in New Haven, we noticed this same shifting of question in the experience of those who were sick and sometimes dying in the hospital. The question posed by the believing sick person to God, to the chaplain, and to themselves was, "Why me?" What is this thing between you and me that I am the one who suffers? God does not answer the question, but lets us struggle with it in solidarity with one another. The chaplain and family are frightened by the question not only because they cannot answer it but also because they themselves are struggling with their own question to God, "Why not me?" Sometimes they fear sickness of others and want to get away from it and conceal it from themselves and the person. Other times they feel guilt that they are well and the person about whom they care is so sick. God does not answer this question either. Yet the experience of those who have been through such suffering in faith is that ultimately the ego, self-centered questions of "Why me?" and "Why not me?" give way unexpectedly to

"Who, me?" This is the response to God's questioning to us, and the discovery that we are called to be faithful in living out our relationship to God in the midst of our situation, for God promises to be present with us in our suffering (Ex. 3:12; Rom. 8:31-39).[9]

God decides to be partner with us, but how do we practice the liberating presence of God in Christ as partner in our lives? Perhaps we can catch a glimpse of this form of spirituality by looking at the way the man called Legion began his new history. We do not know whether the incident of the drowning of the pigs is based on an actual event or is part of an old Jewish folktale that makes a joke of the Gentiles losing all their "unclean swine" (Mark 5:11-13).[10] But the action seems to be intended to demonstrate that a new beginning is made in a definitive way. There is no turning back for the man who had called himself Legion. His story is now all mixed up with that of Jesus of Nazareth no matter what. For him this *is* the jubilee year of liberation and he is free to begin again. The man practices the presence of God in his life by wanting to share the story of Jesus' action for others. At first he thinks that this means going with Jesus, but he soon finds out that it means the difficult task of living out the story and sharing it among his own people (vs. 18-20).

Jesus points away from himself and makes the man the subject of his own new history. The man has discovered his new identity and worth and now he is to work out that liberation in fear and trembling.[11] His freedom for others as a witness to what Christ has done for him is not necessarily going to be easy, if the reaction of the townspeople to the loss of their property and to his sudden recovery is an indication (vs. 14-17). They consider Jesus a public danger and beg him to leave, and they might very well have mixed feelings about their "neighbor" who will now live among them. Their view of reality may be that *their* pigs are more valuable than *his* life, and they may be disturbed by the message of this madman turned evangelist. In our own world we know that God's New Math is subversive of social structures that intend to keep people in chains, and to prevent them from knowing that in God a new beginning is possible. In some places any disturbance is resisted for the sake of order. In Argentina, for instance, the teaching of new math in the schools was recently banned because it encouraged doubt about the authority of the traditional ruling figures.

"In the teaching of modern mathematics the postulates of formal logic are denied. This opens up a dangerous channel for subversive action," claimed the Argentinian magazine *Confirmade* recently.[12]

Mark's story tells us, however, that the Gerasenes were more open to the new evangelist. He is able to carry forward the practice of his spirituality of liberation by sharing his story with others who receive the unexpected news gladly. The clue for us is not that of success, but rather the willingness to show and tell the presence of Christ and his story in our lives so that others may experience it as a calling to partnership.

As Jesus was stepping into the boat, the man who had been possessed begged, "Let me please go with you!" But Jesus had another plan. "I appoint you an evangelist," he said. "Go home, to your folk, there where you belong and show and tell them what the Lord has done for you. Spread the rumor of God, how kind God was." This he did. The man went through the "Ten-Town area" . . ., telling that Jesus had become the beginning of his [new] history. And all who heard it, how surprised they were! Do you know what they said? "MY GOD!"[13]

PARTNERSHIP SPIRITUALITY

Spirituality is our response to the presence of God's Spirit in our lives. This presence is the way God interferes in our lives so we may become partners in God's liberating actions. The practice of the presence of the Spirit includes many of the same aspects of the Christian life that have sustained the church in every age, such as Bible study, prayer, meditation, participation in a community of Word and Sacrament, sharing in gifts of the Spirit, and service of the neighbor.[14] The focus of spirituality of liberation, however, is that of partnership in situations of oppression. From this perspective the building up into the body of Christ is a growth in sharing in the suffering of Christ as well as learning to give an account of hope on the long march in the wilderness (Eph. 4:11-14). This form of spirituality involves a Christian mysticism of partnership. Johannes Metz has pointed out that this type of mysticism does not proceed by denial of the world and flight from it in order to rise to unity with God. Rather, it proceeds by "flight 'forward' with the world" and finds "that direct experience of God which it seeks precisely in daring to imitate the unconditional involvement of the divine love for [humanity]."[15] It lets itself be drawn into the descent of God's love to the least of the brothers and sisters of Christ (Matt. 25:32-46).

Partners in Suffering

For those who find themselves in a situation of dehumanization like that of the Gerasene demoniac, the story of God's deliverance may be the source of strength in the struggle for liberation. As Camilo Torres reminds us, "The New Testament contains not opium, but dynamite."[16] Because God has decided to be with us as Liberator at the center of all our relationships, we find a source of identity and hope that no one can take from us. This enables us to move from apathy, or denial of the situation, toward removing the social, psychological, or physical dimensions of suffering. According to Dorothee Soelle,

> The word suffering expresses first the duration and intensity of a pain and then the multidimensionality that roots the suffering in the physical and social sphere.[17]

In the world of old creation there is much suffering that cannot be removed. In such a situation the most important thing for Christians is whom we serve in the suffering.[18] As we saw in the discussion of the question "Why me?" asked by patients in the hospital, the question changed to a response to God of "Who, me?" when they wrestled with the meaning of their faith. Both the victim of the suffering and the partners in the suffering are called to serve God in and through the suffering. This service does not remove the struggle, but it points us toward a solidarity with God and others that is very important to those who want to "keep on keepin' on" because it brings meaning to a situation that otherwise might be one of meaningless endurance.

It is not necessary to look for suffering as part of the

spirituality of liberation, for it comes to us in the course of a life of faithfulness. Jesus was crucified because he was just "tending to business." The business he was about was God's, and it led him to confront the power structures of his society which were set up to sustain social, political, and economic oppression and religious marginalization. In claiming God's intention of justice he shared the plight of the victims of injustice. When we take up our cross and follow Christ, it is not necessary to look for suffering, because following Christ leads us to be advocates of our neighbors in need and to be troublemakers within the social, political, and economic structures that bring social, psychological, and physical suffering. Spiritual liberation is founded, not on "cheap grace" or "cheap hope," but on the confidence that God has delivered us and set us free to serve others and to bear the cost.[19]

It is necessary to learn from suffering. We can learn the ways we are responsible to work against the injustice that brings so much unnecessary suffering into our world. We can also learn the ways people grow in Christian spirituality as they share as partners in suffering. Dorothee Soelle has suggested in her book entitled *Suffering* that there are phases of suffering through which people move toward liberation. These are phases of conscientization not unlike the ones described in Chapter 2 for the process of changing consciousness of partnership.[20] The first phase, *mute suffering,* finds us speechless as we experience total helplessness and dehumanization. In such a situation of extreme pain, sickness, or despair life contracts and concentrates only on the pain itself. We are isolated from the world and other people. The second phase, *lamenting suffering,* moves away from uncomprehending suffering by finding a language to express how we feel. As in the laments and the cries of the psalmists, we express our situation and protest it to God and to those around us. This results in confrontation with those we perceive as responsible for our suffering and in shared communication among those who share our lot. This phase gradually gives way to a third one, that of *changing suffering,* as communication builds solidarity between us and we begin to organize in whatever way we can to resist the cause of the suffering. "I consider the stage of lament," says Dorothee Soelle,

> to be an indispensable step on the way to the third stage, in which liberation and help for the unfortunate can be organized. The way leads out of isolated suffering through communication (by lament) to the solidarity in which change occurs.[21]

As with other changes of consciousness and action there is much conflict, pain, and ambiguity involved in these phases, yet they do point toward the possibility of partnership in suffering as God grants us the strength to transform it. These phases of suffering are to be seen in situations of extreme social suffering in a concentration camp as well as in situations of physical and psychological suffering. Persons who are imprisoned, for instance, sometimes resign themselves, giving up hope, withdrawing into themselves and waiting to die. Others work to stay alive by the sharing of pain and lament, and still others by organizing in any way possible to help one another to resist. Those who find their lives imprisoned by the systemic structures of racism, sexism, or classism also respond in these different ways, often discovering how to work out their liberation only as they begin to hear their situation described or named in the laments of others. The same sort of process is experienced in times of sickness or death.

In my own case I experienced this change of consciousness not only as I confronted my situation of sexist oppression but also as I confronted the loss of sight in one eye which was due to a freak accident. At first the trauma of the accident and the pain blocked out my full comprehension of the situation. It was as though my mind did not permit me to process anything but very small and immediate bits of information. As I began to recover I became very much preoccupied with my infirmity, constantly talking about it and figuring out ways to reduce the pain, fear, and discomfort. In general I was very hard to live with and anything but mute! As the pain receded and I began to recover, I discovered that my situation was more serious than my preoccupied brain had been willing to imagine. Yet in knowing the problems more fully I also had the emotional resources and ability to share with others that provided a basis for working to improve my situation and working to learn from it.

Analysis of my own experience helped me to learn how to be partner with others in suffering. I discovered that pain and suffering cut one off from others and reduce one's world to one place and one hour or day at a time. This helped me to see that persons in situations of oppression and suffering are also likely to find their world and their understanding of reality greatly constricted.[22] In this situation they need other partners who share with them and work to bring the situation to language and to move it toward the possibility of change. The key to changing consciousness in suffering is the partnership that makes these changes possible. First, the partnership of God present with the person suffering gives the hope needed for just one little step as well as for any larger changes. Second, the partnership of those who share in bringing about social, psychological, and physical cure is key for those who find themselves helpless, dependent, and easily dehumanized in hospital settings as well as in prisons or ghettos. Third, the partnership of those who share in the naming of the situation and help to articulate the groaning and need is a gift from God, who is present through them. Finally, partnership in solidarity among those who face the suffering together and try to change it or to bear it enables the suffering to be transformed as a sign of New Creation in the midst of the old and groaning world.

An example of the importance of partnership in suffering is the hospice movement in this country and abroad. This movement is growing rapidly in the United States, where there are over five hundred organizations with more than eighty-five who have already begun to see patients.[23] It is no wonder that the program is popular, because it develops a partnership in health care for those who are terminally ill. The Hospice Home Care Team involves physicians, nurses, a social worker, a pastoral care counselor, consultants, trained volunteers, and the families of the patient. The program seeks to control the symptoms of the patients who have limited life expectancy so that they can remain at home with their families. The entire team works to make the process of dying a human and humane process of continuing support and growth. Partnership in the process of death and bereavement is not only a means of empowering dying persons and their families to cope with their own suffering, it is a sign to the modern health care system that there are more human and less expensive ways to provide care that treats the person and not just the disease.

We do not look for suffering, but with God's grace we can learn from it. One of the gifts of the Spirit that comes to us out of such situations is that of wisdom. A small example of this can be seen in my own experience and that of others that a serious operation will lead to a new perspective on life. It seems to teach us to value life itself and our partners in that life, rather than worrying about little things. The effect of facing death is that other things are not so important.[24] Blacks learned long ago that suffering produces "soul power" and I guess that this is what I am trying to describe. It is a perspective on life that knows what is important and finds strength and courage for that from God and from sisters and brothers in whose lives God has interfered in some very inconvenient ways. What is important is the quality of our lives as we keep on the journey with others, for others, toward God's future. This impossible journey has become possible for us because God has heard our groaning and decided to be with us in the midst of the suffering.

Theology in the Wilderness

In 1962 a popular book on ministry in the East Harlem Protestant Parish was published with the title *Come out the Wilderness*.[25] Those of us who lived and worked in East Harlem did not like the book, because it tried to picture the work there as a success story. It failed to see that hope springs in the wilderness, not out of success, but out of the discovery that the Lord is present with us even in that situation. Spirituality is related, not to success, but to faithfulness. As we saw in the story of the man called Legion, spirituality includes a willingness to show and tell the presence of Christ and his story in our lives so that others may experience it as a calling to partnership in New Creation. It is the articulation of that presence on the journey toward liberation that we hear in the black spiritual "How did you feel when you come out the wilderness?" In the midst of slavery the people answered,

We feel like a-shoutin' as we come out the wilderness,
Leanin' on the Lord, . . . Who died on Calvary.[26]

The situation of suffering and oppression calls for theological reflection on the way the Lord is with us in that context. By naming and articulating the meaning of that situation we can be part of the process of changing it. This is why liberation theologies see their task as the articulation of hope against hope on the wilderness journey toward the Promised Land of New Creation. They speak from the perspective of the victim and, therefore, emphasize judgment for the victimizer and grace for the victim. For example, a working paper of the Christian Conference of Asia entitled "Let My People Go" declares:

> Our Asian consciousness begins in the awareness of being victims. The centuries of exploitation in the colonial days before our political independence, and today the continuing economic exploitation of our people and our resources, determine our present history. . . . It is of peoples such as ourselves that God's cry is made, "let my people go."[27]

In the effort to articulate the lament as well as the hope, liberation theologies try to take up issues that can best represent the voice of people in contexts of suffering. This calls for the development of the *art of anticipation* in order to understand the ways God's promise breaks into our lives in the present. At the same time it calls for the development of a *collective spirituality* that draws strength from that promise to deal with the world politically, using all the sociopolitical tools possible in action and reflection for social change. In the context of struggle, *accountability* becomes an issue, not just of academic integrity and doctrinal orthodoxy but also of responsibility before God with the community of the oppressed. The theologies strive for an understanding of *the bias of God's justice* in upholding the victims rather than looking for a basis of objectivity or neutrality. They seek out the *wisdom of God* that is buried deep in the collective consciousness and soul of God's people rather than depending on demonstrations of intellectual scholarship. In the light of this shift in perspective it is no wonder that liberation theologies are often seen as "nontheologies." They are identified with the "nonpersons" in society. They begin out of a contextual, sociopolitical base and not out of doctrine or philosophy. And the theologies themselves are "practical." They use tools of critical reflection to articulate the meaning of suffering and the hope for liberation rather than the meaning of doubt and the hope for belief.

Much of the ferment of changing perspectives and methods of theology can be seen in ecumenical gatherings such as those of Faith and Order in the World Council of Churches and the National Council of Churches. Here established white, Western male theologians are joined by Third and Fourth World theologians in seeking to find out how to give an account of the hope of Christ.[28] Often the process breaks down because professional theologians do not yet know how to be partners in a pluralistic setting when the participants do not accept abstract truth as necessarily more universal than incarnated truth. Theologians engaged in developing action/reflection in wilderness situations need time to develop theology in their own context, while those among the "fleshpots of Egypt" need time to shift their own perceptions of reality.

Third World theologians and women are often still in the stage of rejecting the old ways of thinking and exorcising their self-image of inferiority. They have much work to do in making use of the "spoils of the Egyptians" in order to fashion a new life in the wilderness (Ex. 3:21-22). Just as the new social reality of the tribes of Israel brought forth a new understanding of the religion of Yahweh, the new social reality of those who are on their freedom journey presses them to new understandings of religious faith. What often happens when professional theologians gather from these different contexts to seek consensus on an issue is that the two different methodologies are combined. The group begins inductively with stories and questions drawn out of action/reflection, and then they seek out the doctrines and traditions that can be used as the answers. This does not provide a critical basis for systematic theologies that are deductive in method, and it does not provide a means of carrying through on the inductive methodology of liberation theologies. From the point of view of the latter it is necessary to keep the questions and the story open as the theology continues to develop on the wilderness journey. The stories need to be interpreted out of further investigations of biblical stories and their meaning which illuminates the actions, rather than by abstractions out of the actions that stop the unfolding process of action/reflection.

Women who are in the struggles to articulate theology in the wilderness share the same issues and perspectives, but their context is even more complex. All women find themselves in the wilderness of sexism where they are assigned to an "underclass" by birth. Yet some suffer from double or "triple jeopardy." They may have as many as three oppressions to deal with if they are women who are black or Third World and who are second-class citizens in the church as laity.[29] Other women find that they are status inconsistent in sharing the privilege of their husbands, family, or nation. They are divided in their consciousness within and between themselves by virtue of this mixture of roles. They are often beset with paralyzing guilt because they have internalized the guilt of inferiority projected on them by their masters, and at the same time they know themselves to be guilty as participants in the affluence of an oppressor society. In some ways this is not unlike the situation of other persons who know themselves to be confronted by a call to justice which is both liberating and judging in their lives.

Feminist theologians have sought to articulate the groaning of women and to build solidarity among those working to anticipate the meaning of new human wholeness. These professional and nonprofessional theologians are informed by emerging feminist consciousness and culture expressed especially in new life-styles and in music, art, and literature. Of particular interest to women is the development of space for growth and wholeness. Women have a great need for "room to breathe" when they are living in a dominant culture which exploits and denies their wholeness as human beings. Women, like other oppressed communities, have sought to create institutions where such space is possible so that theological reflection and action can spring out of small anticipation of new community.

Examples of this in the field of theology have been gathered together in a book called *Your Daughters Shall Prophesy: Feminist Alternatives in Theological Education.* In a collective writing process a group of women have reflected on some of the "experiences women have had in searching out new ways of working in the context of theological education."[30] They discuss the possibilities of "alternative space" in women's centers, women's projects and research, as well as alternative seminary experiences such as the summer Seminary Quarter at Grailville, Ohio. This is not a success story, for it is full of problems from lack of power, lack of access to resources, and lack of participation in the decision-making structures of theological education. But it does tell of how women discovered their solidarity in the common struggle of women and other movements for liberation.[31] Together they affirmed the importance of theological reflection for collective naming and re-imaging as well as in action for systemic change.

Women, like other oppressed groups, need room to develop their own identity and process of theological reflection. This already happens at the margins of institutions, in extension programs, in formal and informal continuing education, and in action/reflection and support groups. As long as the theological institutions are dominated by a pedagogy *of* the oppressors they will continue to be largely blind to the contribution being made by marginal groups to the renewal of theology, and the institutions themselves will continue to be unhealthy for women and for new forms of partnership.[32] In this situation women will need space of their own where they can develop their own theology in the wilderness and discover the ways that the Spirit of God is breaking into their midst.

PEDAGOGY FOR PARTNERSHIP

Like other oppressed groups, women discover that spirituality of liberation is not just a part of their life to be added on to other activities. Rather, it is *all* of life when that life is lived as a response to Christ's call to service in the midst of suffering humanity. From this perspective the struggle out of bondage is not just a problem to be solved.[33] It is a new world to be created through partnership with God and with those who build solidarity in the midst of groaning creation. The unexpected presence of God's love in our lives makes that partnership possible and encourages us to share in God's action by developing a *pedagogy for partnership.*

As I pointed out in Chapter 5, each context calls for a different style of education for partnership. What is helpful for discovering solidarity in groaning among members of oppressor groups may not be helpful in building solidarity among the oppressed. This was brought home to me in 1980 when I attended a workshop on sexism at the National Event for Joint Educational Development in San Antonio, Texas. We were going through the five movements of Thomas Groome's "Shared Praxis Approach" in order to learn how to address issues of sexism and how to use that approach in teaching and learning. I found that the method seemed to be helpful for raising consciousness in a rather neutral way for men in the group, but it did not seem to challenge the women to new actions and insights regarding their own oppression. There are, of course, many reasons this may have happened, but the experience underlined for me the importance of looking at the need for a specific pedagogy for each context.

Persons in oppressor groups who are searching out a new identity in solidarity with groaning creation need a pedagogy for the oppressor, but those in oppressed groups who reach the identity stage of consciousness have a different need. Their consciousness has been raised through what Freire calls "pedagogy of the oppressed," but they still need to develop the depth of spirituality that will sustain them for the long journey. It would seem to me that this would call for development of a pedagogy *for* partnership. It is not yet a pedagogy *of* partners, because we have not yet arrived at the ability to be full partners among our own group or with other groups. The goal is, of course, full partnership and mutuality in Christ that sets us free for others. In this realization of God's New Creation, pedagogies will be put out of business (Jer. 31:33-34).

Meanwhile a pedagogy for partnership may help to provide clues for developing a spirituality of liberation among the oppressed. Those who search for freedom from oppression even as they continue to journey in the wilderness may also find the impossible possibility of freedom for partnership as they respond to God's call in solidarity with one another. In discussing these six clues for acting our way into partnership, I will use examples drawn from my experience with a group of professional women related to or working in church, education, or social change organizations. This group grew out of the New York Task Force on Women in Changing Institutions which was related to a World Council of Churches study project.[34] The interracial group with white laywomen predominating decided to form The Ad Hoc Group on Racism, Sexism, and Classism (RSAC) in 1973 as a means of continuing action/reflection and support for women in institutions that they would like to change. In its very ordinary and rather chaotic monthly meetings RSAC seems to me to provide an example of pedagogy for partnership.

Freedom from Oppression
How do we "keep on keepin' on" in the wilderness? There are times when we don't "feel like a-shoutin' " even though we are "leanin' on the Lord." Freedom from oppression is a gift of God's Spirit, but it is often lived out in difficult and inconspicuous situations where we have to work out actions of partnership that prevent us from burning out or selling out to the existing reality of old creation. In the moments of discouragement with ourselves and with the slowness of change in church and society we need to nurture what Ursala Niebuhr has called "the discipline of non-fulfillment."[35] In the pedagogy for partnership we can begin this task by developing the skills of cultivating advent shock, sharing tasks, and learning to be bicultural.

In the discussion of clues to God's New Math in Chapter 1, advent shock was described as maladjustment with the present because of the longed-for future. The forces of systemic oppression are such that *cultivating advent shock* is essential for those who do not want to give up hope. By remaining open to God's promised future we allow the reality of New Creation to enter our present reality (II Cor. 5:16-21). In my ministry in East Harlem the Advent season was one of my favorite times. The reason for this was that it was possible to anticipate the meaning of Christmas and to celebrate the coming of Christ with people who found that poverty had transformed Christmas into a time of frustration. Amid the affluent and commerical aspects of Christmas, they found themselves with debts and degrading handouts. A way to negate this negative was to invite children and adults alike to celebrate the coming of Christ in story, song, and service long before the Christmas rush so that Christ's presence in our midst could interfere with business as usual.

The art of anticipation is a survival skill and not just an optional method of biblical interpretation, because anticipating God's intention for our lives leads us to seek out the partnership with others that belongs to New Creation. Acting as if we are already partners in spite of the "not yet" quality of our daily lives is a way that we can grow in partnership. We cultivate advent shock not only by thinking and acting from the other end but also by sharing in the development of new styles of life, art, and action that create a counterculture which supports more egalitarian relationships and which values the gifts of persons apart from their income or social status. In RSAC we have developed a new tradition in our life together by holding an *advance* rather than a *retreat* each spring. The time for evaluation and looking forward to the future is a time for cultivating advent shock. People literally advance from the New York area to my house in Connecticut in order to be disturbed! As we begin to speak of the present pain and the horizon of the future we are almost always surprised by a new agenda demanding our attention. Recently that agenda became solidarity with women struggling for justice in places like Korea and El Salvador. Somehow God's Spirit seems to interfere with orderly plans and we hear challenges regarding the way we have shortchanged the issues of racism or human rights. Thus together we find new ways to be maladjusted with injustice and to take some small steps for change.

Those who are in situations of oppression learn to be partners by *sharing tasks*. This is essential for getting the job done when you have fewer resources and lack access to. finances, power, or knowledge. It is also essential because common action in personal or public life provides a "third thing" around which partnership can be formed. Mutual building up happens most frequently around a task. People discover the gifts of the Spirit, not in the abstract, but in the action of community as they carry out God's agenda of mending creation (Eph. 4:1-16). It is the tasks that make it possible to share life together even when people are very different from each other. In the struggle to create partnership in situations of oppression, commitment to a shared goal or action can help to contradict the way that pressures from above lead us to shortchange one another in terms of time and caring support.[36]

Along with personal ties it is the sharing of tasks that keeps the "nonorganization" of RSAC from falling apart. When I moved to the New Haven area after my husband died, I thought the group would disband, because it had been meeting in our apartment. But each year the group has decided to continue and members have volunteered to take responsibility for hospitality and leadership. Olga Paspalas has continued to maintain the only centralized part of the group, a mailing list kept in the office of Emily Gibbes, Associate General Secretary of the National Council of Churches. The meetings that are particularly helpful are usually ones in which the persons leading are highly invested in a task and look to the group for mutual support and reflection on their action. We found the most solidarity in our groaning when we discussed specific tasks such as how to organize a visible presence of Feminists of Faith at the Houston National Women's Conference for International Woman's Year, or what to do about changing a person's job, or about the failure of an important church program. Our diversity became an asset for reflecting together as partners on the alternatives for the tasks and problems at hand.

Those who are members of oppressed groups live in culture shock. They live in the survival culture of their own group, but at the same time are linked to the "normative" culture of the dominant group. Cognitive dissonance is a way of life. The reality described in most church, school, government, and media communications is not the reality that they experience in their own lives. In such a setting one can cope by ignoring the culture of the dominant group and withdrawing into a mental or physical ghetto, but for those who want to take steps to name and to change the contradictions of the world around them, *learning to be bicultural* is essential. A person who is bicultural is in the identity stage of consciousness but is aware that no perception of reality is the whole truth, and that it is necessary to know the perception, speech, and action of the different cultures in order to transform life into a continuing journey toward freedom (Ex. 3). The danger of this is "selling out." One becomes so good at making it in the system and "collecting the spoils of the Egyptians" that the reality of oppression that is faced by most people in one's own racial, sexual, economic, age, or health group is forgotten.[37] Yet it is possible to live out the reality of one's own freedom in the midst of oppressive systems when the skills of living in both worlds are cultivated. In this case one learns to understand each reality more critically and more deeply because one has the possibility of standing "outside" of them and looking for aspects of both worlds that can contribute to the humanization of society. Partners are very important for developing and for correcting these perceptions.

Christians become bicultural because they seek to live out the life-style and history of Jesus Christ in their own culture and historical context. Women and Third World persons can also become bicultural as they recognize the value of their own cultural expressions and life-styles and begin to view their experience of the dominant culture with critical eye. Thus, for instance, in theological education for women and blacks there needs to be an opportunity to learn about one's own culture, history, worship styles, and role models as well as to learn the tools for biblical, theological, historical, and practical reflection. In RSAC the women very frequently work to develop skills of social analysis that can help them support one another in the white, male-dominated structures of the church. One small example of this was a meeting in which the group shared in action/reflection on "Working for Social Justice in the Bureaucracy."[38] At the same time, they share in the development of liturgy and worship experiences that combine the new consciousness and cultural forms of women with such traditional forms as foot washing and agape meals.

Freedom for Partnership

Liberation from oppression is a long journey that calls for the development of spirituality of liberation as we respond to God's interference in our lives. The presence of Christ at the center of our existence sets us free to become partners and places us together with others in a community of freedom. In this context a pedagogy for partnership is important to us as we seek to "stand fast" in the freedom of Christ (Gal. 5:1). As we learn to work out this freedom for partnership, three clues that may be of help are building solidarity, challenging our perceptions, and celebrating marginality.

Oppressed groups do not necessarily stick together. They need to *build solidarity* in their struggles in order to prevent the pressures from society from crushing them and splitting them apart. The dominant culture tells members of the subordinate groups that they not only are to have a subordinate role but also a low opinion of themselves and their abilities. This in turn causes them to distrust themselves and others. In competing for the crumbs of society, people turn on one another and often allow themselves to be convinced that their group or other subordinate groups are responsible for scarcity of resources or jobs in society. For instance, women are supposed to be taking away jobs from black males, but no one notices that it is the white males who control the jobs that both blacks and women would want. Often groups believe these myths and do not recognize that, like the tribes of Israel, they have been set free to form a coalition or solidarity of those who work for a just and representative society. The oppressed are called to solidarity in groaning and in journeying toward freedom (Luke 4:16-30). This takes place as groups take time to listen to one another along the road, to speak truth to one another as it is needed for staying on the road, and to act in support of one another in the wilderness.

Supportiveness and caring are not separate from action for social and institutional change. One person reflecting on her experience in a women's clergy support group told me that she was surprised to discover this. The group had avoided politics until elections came around and they had to decide whom they would support for church offices. In this case the political process was very much a factor in developing partnership because support of someone meant working for conditions in which she could grow toward her full potential.[39] In RSAC, support has been related to action the other way around. The women are so very active and overinvolved that the group tries to develop skills of listening and a network of communication that is there as people need it without making any great demands. Solidarity in this case includes being there as a group when people need the group, but making it clear that they don't have to attend in order to be partners. Solidarity extends to those who do not come to the meeting, and the group is open to all women, including those who just want to drop in even for an hour or so. The other form of solidarity that needs constant work is that between various groups represented in the interlocking oppression of racism, sexism, and classism. Often the group fails in this wider task, but it continues to struggle for this broader solidarity in groaning.

Pedagogy for partnership includes the development of skills in *challenging our perceptions*. Reflection on bicultural experience is very helpful in developing a critical awareness of various alternative views of reality. Thinking from the other end presses us to view things from the perspective of God's promise and God's great reversals (Jer. 31:15-34). But these actions need to be developed further in relation to challenging our perceptions of reality. People who are in subordinate positions in society need to question their own views of reality, but they often do not have access to enough information, or their views have been contracted by the situation of oppression in which they find themselves. In order for us to clarify the real basis of bonding with others, it is important that we be suspicious of our own motives and ideas as well as those of others. We can develop this suspicion by reading or listening to the conflicting views and analyses of a variety of persons as well as by opening ourselves to the challenge of God's Spirit through prayer, study, reflection, and sharing in communities of faith.

In developing a healthy suspicion of our own perceptions, we need to allow ourselves to be vulnerable to others who share our situation and our commitments so that they can speak words of both judgment and grace as they are needed, and can share stories and advice about similar circumstances. Developing a sense of humor and playfulness is important for the cultivation of such wisdom, for things do not seem quite so serious or oppressive if we can treat them with a sense of humor. Robert McAfee Brown claims that humor is a gift of the Spirit, a "saving grace" that enables us to see things in proper proportion.[40] Through such humor God challenges our own perceptions of reality and opens us up to new possibilities of partnership in liberating action.

In RSAC there is a great deal of challenging one another's perceptions that goes on in formal critiques of social structures and of our work for change, but probably the greatest testing comes from the give-and-take of persons of different age, race, and background who challenge one another by their styles of life and work as much as by what they say. Humor, playfulness, and vulnerability keep the ferment of the challenging process continuing so that facts have a human face as they challenge us to change. Much of this happens in unexpected ways because of the "calculated inefficiency" of the group. A lot of the nonorganization provides space for surprise parties, visitors from abroad, and personal or institutional crises to change the agendas. It is hoped that this helps develop an openness to what the Spirit might be saying to us in the midst of this process.

Many persons experience their own marginality in an institution or a social setting: persons and groups that are old or young, sick or poor, nonwhite, nonordained, female, or gay, just to name a few. Yet those who are responding to God's call to journey toward freedom will find that strength for partnership grows when we *celebrate marginality*. God has identified with the misfits of the world and encourages us to become marginal to structures that operate by standards of domination, injustice, and competition. It was no accident that the man who met the demoniac outside the city among the tombs was also the one who died outside the city on a cross (Mark 5:1-20). Marginality is to be celebrated not because the structures of old creation are good, but because God is present in the places of rejection. This celebration of God's presence in turn frees us to see ways in which the periphery can be turned into a position of strength and blessing. It can be a good place to be if the person or groups are sufficiently connected to a particular institution that they have the possibility of interacting with it to bring about change.

On the margin there is more freedom not to conform, and more space in which to develop alternative life-styles, identity, and culture. Never a comfortable place to be, the margin of society may well still be the best place for those who wish to be an exodus people. In my own life I have known for many years that I was marginal in the church and in educational institutions where I worked, but I was only able to celebrate this and turn it around into a clue for partnership and solidarity when I claimed the margin as a good place to be along with my black and Puerto Rican neighbors in East Harlem, and along with my sisters on the edge of Yale University. In RSAC this marginality is celebrated as a free space in which to develop partnership and build solidarity so that we may find strength for working to open up the institutions in which we work so that all persons may be free to participate. RSAC is an ad hoc group with no budget. Its marginality corresponds to the position of many of its members and so negates the negative of that position. For them it is right in the center of God's small reversals of life. When there are places to go such as this group where we are not marginal we find new and creative ways to share in God's intention that God's will be done *on earth,* so that all marginal people are welcomed as full members of the New Creation.

Education for partnership happens as we invite one another to be partners together in God's liberating action. Pedagogy for partnership is one form of this partnering process that provides clues for building solidarity among those who share in the groaning of creation. Here we find a new focus of relationship in the history of Jesus Christ as God's Spirit interferes in our lives and sets us free for many unexpected tasks and roles. We are no longer surprised to see a madman turned evangelist, or women turned into warriors, or even men sharing in the groaning and pain of childbirth as part of God's unexpected action (Mark 5:18-20; Jer. 31:22; Rom. 8:22-23).

No one knows what full partnership in God's New Creation

will look like, but we have caught a glimpse of this possibility in the story of Jesus of Nazareth. Those who become partners in his story with suffering humanity seem always surprised when he speaks to them in the center of their lives. They respond, "Who, me?" when he calls them (Matt. 25:37-40). Yet they discover Christ's presence with them as partners just because they have been worrying about the mending of God's creation so that it might be set free from bondage.

> I consider that whatever we suffer now cannot be compared to all the splendor as yet not revealed, which is in store for us. The created universe is waiting on tiptoe for the children of God, to show what they are. In fact, the fondest dream of the universe is to catch a glimpse of real live children! (Rom. 8:18-19)[41]

NEXT QUESTIONS

In the 1960's I received a beautiful print of a poster by Sister Corita for my birthday from my co-workers and close friends, Hal Eads and Faye Edwards. As only friends can do, they had found the perfect picture for me! It said ORNERY in large purple letters written backwards. As I hung up the picture it asked me about the way I sometimes make it hard for others to be partners with me by being stubborn or irritable. Soon the partnership of our interracial Christian community in East Harlem was seriously tested in the struggle for black liberation. In the midst of these events I saw the second row of words in the Corita poster. Written in bright green behind the purple letters were the words HIP DEEP INVOLVEMENT. They asked me about my ability to be partner with the oppressed on the road toward freedom. .

As time brought change, separation, and the challenge of feminism I finally turned to the third row of words in the background of the picture. This was the quote from Rilke that began, "BE PATIENT TOWARD THINGS THAT ARE UNSOLVED IN YOUR HEART AND TRY TO LOVE THE QUESTIONS." It asked me about whether I am open and committed enough to God's partnership in New Creation to live with and love the questions. All these questions are woven into the discussion of education for partnership in this book. Now we are off the picture and off the page, but we are not finished with the questions. We have simply moved them into the background of our own lives where we can find the next questions.

NOTES

1. PARTNERSHIP IN NEW CREATION

1. Unless otherwise indicated, all Bible quotations are from the *Revised Standard Version of the Holy Bible* (Thomas Nelson, 1946, 1952, 1971, 1973). Brackets indicate that I have substituted a word or phrase.

2. *The New English Bible* (Oxford University Press and Cambridge University Press, 1961, 1970). The Greek is literally "If anyone in Christ—a new creation . . ." The male pronoun was added to the text in the RSV, and the King James Version.

3. D. Georgi, "Corinthians, First Letter to the," and "Corinthians, Second Letter to the," in Keith Crim et al. (eds.), *The Interpreter's Dictionary of the Bible*, Supplementary Volume (Abingdon Press, 1976), pp. 180-186. Cited as IDBS.

4. Ibid., pp. 184-185; Wayne Meeks (ed.), *The Writings of St. Paul* (W. W. Norton & Co., 1972), pp. 49-50.

5. Wayne Meeks, *The Writings of St. Paul*, p. 49.

6. Justo L. and Catherine Gunsalus Gonzalez, *Rejoice in Your Savior: A Study Book* (United Methodist Publishing House, 1979), pp. 34-37.

7. Robin Scroggs, *Paul for a New Day* (Fortress Press, 1977), p. 26.

8. Krister Stendahl, *Paul Among Jews and Gentiles* (Fortress Press, 1976) pp. 7-23.

9. Ibid., p. 46.

10. Ibid., p. 31; Scroggs, *Paul for a New Day*, pp. 14-17.

11. James H. Cone, *God of the Oppressed* (Seabury Press, 1975), p. 230.

12. Rosemary Radford Ruether, *Mary—The Feminine Face of the Church* (Westminster Press, 1977), p. 86.

13. *Daily Bible Readings: Inner City Parishes* (The East Harlem Protestant Parish, 1968), p. 21. Drawings by Joseph Papin.

14. Robin Scroggs regards I Cor. 14:33b-36 as a post-Pauline gloss similar in thought to I Tim. 2:11ff. Cf. Robin Scroggs, "Paul and the Eschatological Woman," *Journal of the American Academy of Religion*, Vol. 40 (1972), pp. 283-303; cf. Hans Conzelmann, *First Corinthians* (Fortress Press, 1975), p. 246.

15. Jean Baker Miller, *Toward a New Psychology of Women* (Beacon Press, 1976), pp. 16, 36, 123-124.

16. A. Oepke, "En," *Theological Dictionary of the New Testament*, ed. by Gerhard Kittel and Gerhard Friedrich, tr. and ed. by Geoffrey W. Bromiley (Wm. B. Eerdmans Publishing Co., 10 vols., 1964-1976), Vol. II, pp. 541-542. Cited as TDNT.

17. B. W. Anderson, "Creation," *The Interpreter's Dictionary of the Bible*, ed. by George Arthur Buttrick et al. (Abingdon Press, 1962), Vol. I, p. 732. Cited as IDB. Cf. also W. Foerster, "Ktizo", TDNT, Vol. III, p. 1034.

18. K. Rahner, "Man (Anthropology)," *Sacramentum Mundi*, ed. by Karl Rahner et al. (Herder & Herder, 1969), Vol. III, p. 366.

19. E. Schüssler Fiorenza, "Eschatology of the NT," IDBS, pp. 271-277; cf. Gunther Bornkam, *Paul,* tr. by D. M. Stalker (Harper & Row, 1971), pp. 196-227.

20. Anton Houtepen, "Koinonia and Consensus," *The Ecumenical Review*, Vol. 31, No. 1 (January 1979), pp. 60-63.

21. F. Hauck, "*Koinos,*" TDNT, Vol. III, pp. 804-809.

22. Letty M. Russell, *The Future of Partnership* (Westminster Press, 1979), pp. 17-20, 51-53. Cited as *Partnership.*

23. Justo L. Gonzalez, "Searching for a Liberating Anthropology," *Theology Today*, Vol. 34, No. 4 (January 1978), p. 390.

24. Letty M. Russell, *Human Liberation in a Feminist Perspective—A Theology* (Westminster Press, 1974), pp.

106-109, cited as *Human Liberation*. Cf. Claus Westermann, *Blessing in the Bible and the Life of the Church*, tr. by Keith Crim (Fortress Press, 1978), p. 8.

25. M. Douglas Meeks, "How to Speak of God in an Affluent Society," *The Witness*, Vol. 62, No. 10 (October 1979), p. 8.

26. James Parks Morton, "Listen to the Earth," *Christianity and Crisis*, Vol. 40, No. 1 (Feb. 4, 1980), pp. 10-12.

27. Sister Marie Augusta Neal, "Sociology and Sexuality," *Christianity and Crisis*, Vol. 39, No. 8 (May 14, 1979), pp. 188-122.

28. Elizabeth Dodson Gray, *Why the Green Nigger? Re-Mything Genesis* (Wellesley, Mass.: Roundtable Press, 1979), p. 127.

29. Unit Committee Meeting, Division of Education and Ministry, National Council of the Churches of Christ in the U.S.A., June 11-12, 1980. Cf. Reginald H. Fuller, *Preaching the New Lectionary* (Liturgical Press, 1971).

30. The idea of new grammar was suggested to me by a student at Perkins School of Theology, Dallas, January 1980.

31. Russell, *Partnership*, Ch. 1, "God's Arithmetic," pp. 25-43; cf. Hans-Ruedi Weber, "God's Arithmetic," *Mission Trends, No. 2: Evangelization,* ed. by Gerald H. Anderson and Thomas F. Stransky (Paulist Press, 1975), pp. 64-69. The metaphor of "new math" is suggested by the fact that the teaching of new math in the schools in the U.S.A. met with difficulty just because it was a new way of looking at reality. (Discussion with Mary Boys, September 1980.)

32. Russell, *Partnership*, pp. 18-19.

33. Paul Tillich, *The Courage to Be* (Yale University Press, 1952), 1978 edition, p. 75. This idea was suggested to me by John Britton at Yale Divinity School, December 1978.

34. Alvin Toffler, *Future Shock* (Bantam Books, 1971).

35. Miller, *Toward a New Psychology of Women,* pp. 3-12.

36. Paul Ricoeur, "The Logic of Jesus, the Logic of God," *Christianity and Crisis,* Vol. 39, No. 20 (Dec. 24, 1979), pp. 324-327.

37. Russell, *Partnership,* p. 19.

38. Ted Peters, *Fear, Faith, and the Future: Affirming*

Christian Hope in the Face of Doomsday Prophecies (Augsburg Publishing House, 1980), pp. 120-121.

39. *Sexism in the 1970's—Discrimination Against Women* (Geneva: World Council of Churches, 1974).

40. Miller, *Toward a New Psychology of Women,* p. 4.

41. J. C. Hoekendijk, *The Church Inside Out* (Westminster Press, 1966), p. 23.

2. COMMUNITY OF LEARNING

1. N. A. Dahl, "Ephesians, Letter to the," IDBS, pp. 268-269.

2. Wayne Meeks, *The Writings of St. Paul*, pp. 121-123.

3. Letty M. Russell, "Equipping the Little Saints," *The Adult Teacher*, Vol. 15, No. 5 (May 1962), Methodist Publishing House.

4. Peter Hammond, Yale Divinity School, 1980.

5. Russell, *Partnership*, pp. 120-126.

6. "Baptism," provisional text for submission to Faith and Order Commission, January 1981, Geneva, World Council of Churches, FO/80:2 (February 1980).

7. Marcus Barth, *Ephesians*, Vol. 2, *The Anchor Bible* (Doubleday & Co., 1974), pp. 435-439.

8. Ibid., p. 438.

9. Scroggs, *Paul for a New Day*, pp. 72-74; Stendahl, *Paul Among Jews and Gentiles*, pp. 54-67.

10. Stendahl, *Paul Among Jews and Gentiles,* p. 67.

11. Christy John, "From Oppression to Liberation: Towards a Theology of Liberation in The Church of South India" (Unpublished STM dissertation, Yale Divinity School, 1980), p. 4.

12. Russell, *Partnership*, pp. 26-28.

13. O. Michel, "Oikodome," TDNT, Vol. V, pp. 144-147.

14. P. S. Minear, "Christ, Body of," IDB, Vol. I, p. 571.

15. *Daily Bible Readings: Inner City Parishes*, p. 11.

16. Barth, *Ephesians*, pp. 441, 487.

17. Lois MacDonald, First Congregational Church of West Haven, Connecticut.

18. Ian A. Muirhead, *Education in the New Testament* (Association Press, 1965), p. 48. Cf. Hans-Ruedi Weber,

Jesus and the Children (Geneva: World Council of Churches, 1979).

19. Malcolm S. Knowles, *The Modern Practice of Adult Education: Andragogy Versus Pedagogy* (Association Press, 1972).

20. Henrich Heppe, *Reformed Dogmatics*, tr. by G. T. Thomson (London: George Allen & Unwin, 1950), pp. 530-534. These aspects of faith were described by the Reformers as *fiducia, notitia,* and *assensus.* Cf. Thomas H. Groome, *Christian Religious Education: Sharing Our Story and Vision* (Harper & Row, 1980), pp. 57-66.

21. James W. Fowler, "Faith Development Theory and the Aims of Religious Socialization," *Emerging Issues in Religious Education,* ed. by Gloria Durka and Joanmarie Smith (Paulist Press, 1976), pp. 187-208. Cf. Jim Fowler and Sam Keen, *Life Maps: Conversations on the Journey to Faith,* ed. by Jerome Berryman (Word Books, 1978); James W. Fowler and Robin W. Lovin, *Trajectories in Faith: Five Life Stories* (Abingdon Press, 1980).

22. James W. Fowler, "Stages in Faith: The Structural-Development Approach," *Values and Moral Development,* ed. by Thomas C. Hennessy (Paulist Press, 1976), pp. 175-179, 207-211.

23. Ibid., pp. 183-185; J. Fowler, "Future Christians and Church Education," *Hope for the Church,* ed. by Theodore Runyon (Abingdon Press, 1979), p. 111.

24. Discussion with Andrew Grannell and Sharon Parks at a meeting of Professors of Religious Education on the Eastern Seaboard, Princeton Theological Seminary, April 1980. Cf. Sharon Parks, "Communities as Ministry," *NICM Journal,* Vol. 2, No. 1 (Winter 1977), pp. 74-75.

25. John H. Westerhoff III, *Will Our Children Have Faith?* (Seabury Press, 1976), pp. 89-99. Cf. also the models of Kierkegaard and Tillich in Madonna Kolbenschlag, *Kiss Sleeping Beauty Good-Bye: Breaking the Spell of Feminine Myths and Models* (Doubleday & Co., 1979), pp. 25-28.

26. James W. Fowler, "Stage Six and the Kingdom of God," *Religious Education,* Vol. 75, No. 3 (May-June 1980), pp. 231-248.

27. E. L. Simpson, "Moral Development Research, A

Case Study of Scientific Cultural Bias," *Human Development*, Vol. 17 (1974), pp. 81-106. Cf. Maria Harris, *Portrait of Ministry: Young People and the Church* (Paulist Press, 1980), Chs. 2 and 4; Gabriel Moran, *Education Toward Adulthood* (Paulist Press, 1979), pp. 105-109; Carol Gilligan, *In a Different Voice* (Harvard University Press, 1981).

28. David Shields, "Education for Moral Action," *Religious Education*, Vol. 75, No. 2 (March-April 1980), pp. 129-141. Shields is summarizing work on moral dialogue by Norma Haan at the Institute of Human Development, Berkeley.

29. Fowler, "Stages in Faith," pp. 182, 191.

30. Alfred McBride, "Reaction to Fowler: Fears About Procedure," Hennessy, *Values and Moral Development*, pp. 211-218.

31. Gail Sheehy, *Passages: Predictable Crises in Adult Life* (Bantam Books, 1977), p. 23. Kolbenschlag, *Kiss Sleeping Beauty Good-Bye,* p. 167.

32. Lawrence Kohlberg, "Moral Development and Faith," *Collected Papers in Moral Development* (Harvard Center for Moral Development and Moral Education, 1975).

33. David Steward of Pacific School of Religion refers to this view of development as one that is "spatial" rather than "chronological." Focus is on the interaction among persons in various types of events. Conversation with Steward in Berkeley, California, January 1980.

34. Cf. Chapter 1, section "God's New Math."

35. Cf. especially Fowler, "Locus of Authority," *Life Maps,* pp. 96-97.

36. Fuller, *Preaching the New Lectionary.*

37. Barth, *Ephesians*, pp. 438-439.

38. Letty M. Russell, "Handing On Traditions and Changing the World," *Tradition and Transformation in Religious Education*, ed. by Padraic O'Hare (Religious Education Press, 1979), pp. 73-86; Charles F. Melchert, "What Is the Educational Ministry of the Church?" *Religious Education*, Vol. 73, No. 4 (July -Aug. 1978), pp. 429-439.

39. Rosemary Radford Ruether, *New Woman, New Earth: Sexist Ideologies and Human Liberation* (Seabury Press, 1975), p. 66.

40. Hans Hoekendijk, *Horizons of Hope* (Tidings Press, 1970), p. 30.

41. Letty M. Russell, *Christian Education in Mission* (Westminster Press, 1967), p. 28.

42. Letty M. Russell, "Partnership in Educational Ministry," *Religious Education*, Vol. 74, No. 2 (March-April 1979), pp. 143-146.

43. Gloria Durka, "Modeling Religious Education for the Future," *The Religious Education We Need*, ed. by James Michael Lee (Religious Education Press, 1977), pp. 95-111.

44. James F. White, "The Actions of Worship: Beyond Liturgical Sexism," *The Christian Century*, Vol. 97, No. 17 (May 7, 1980), pp. 521-523.

45. Shannon Clarkson, First Congregational Church of West Haven, Connecticut.

46. Robert K. Greenleaf, *Servant Leadership: A Journey Into the Nature of Legitimate Power and Greatness* (Paulist Press, 1977), pp. 7-10.

3. EDUCATION AS EXODUS

1. David Drake (Unpublished report, Yale Divinity School, 1980). Used by permission.

2. Hoekendijk, *The Church Inside Out*, pp. 188-189.

3. Peter C. Hodgson, *New Birth of Freedom* (Fortress Press, 1976), pp. 334-335. Cone, *God of the Oppressed*, pp. 163-194.

4. Muirhead, *Education in the New Testament*, p. 51.

5. Russell, *Human Liberation*, p. 25.

6. Walter Brueggemann, *The Prophetic Imagination* (Fortress Press, 1978), p. 17; cf. Norman K. Gottwald, *The Tribes of Yahweh* (Orbis books, 1979), pp. 696-697.

7. Bruce C. Birch and Larry L. Rasmussen, *The Predicament of the Prosperous* (Westminster Press, 1978), pp. 83-85.

8. Dorothee Soelle, "Resistance Toward a First World Theology," *Christianity and Crisis*, Vol. 39, No. 12 (July 23, 1979), pp. 178-182; cf. Frederick Herzog, *Justice Church: The New Function of the Church in North American Christianity* (Orbis Books, 1980), pp. 93-94.

9. Gerhard E. Lenski and Jean Lenski, *Human Societies*,

3d ed. (McGraw-Hill Book Co., 1977), p. 56.

10. Martin Noth, *Exodus, A Commentary*, tr. by J. S. Bowden, The Old Testament Library (Westminster Press, 1962), p. 42.

11. Brevard S. Childs, *The Book of Exodus*, A Critical, Theological Commentary, The Old Testament Library (Westminster Press, 1974), pp. 56-60.

12. Gerhard von Rad, *Old Testament Theology*, Vol. I, tr. by D. M. G. Stalker (Harper & Row, 1962), pp. 181-182.

13. Gottwald, *The Tribes of Yahweh*, p. 682. He is quoting Frank M. Cross, *Canaanite Myth and Hebrew Epic* (Harvard University Press, 1973), pp. 65-71. Cf. Childs, *The Book of Exodus.*

14. J. A. Sanders, "Hermeneutics," IDBS, pp. 402-407.

15. Abraham J. Heschel, *The Prophets* (Harper & Row, 1962), p. 22.

16. Dwayne Heubner, "Toward a Remaking of Curricular Language," *Heightened Consciousness, Cultural Revolution, and Curriculum Theory*, ed. by William Pinar (McCutchan Publishing Corp., 1974), p. 52; cf. Mary C. Boys, *Biblical Interpretation in Religious Education* (Religious Education Press, 1980), p. 229; Groome, *Christian Religious Education*, pp. 18-19.

17. Krister Stendahl, "God Worries About Every Ounce of Creation," *Harvard Divinity Bulletin*, Vol. 9, No. 5 (June/July 1979), p. 5.

18. Gabriel Moran, *Design for Religion* (Herder & Herder, 1970), p. 21.

19. James Michael Lee, "Toward a New Era: A Blueprint for Positive Action," *The Religious Education We Need*, ed. by Lee, p. 121.

20. Harold William Burgess, *An Invitation to Religious Education* (Religious Education Press, 1975), p. 21.

21. Paulo Freire, *Pedagogy of the Oppressed* (Herder & Herder, 1970), pp. 75-76.

22. David S. Steward and Margaret Steward, "Action-Reflection-Action: Our Embedment in the World," *Parish Religious Education*, ed. by Maria Harris (Paulist Press, 1978), pp. 87-90.

23. Letty M. Russell, "Education as Exodus," *Mid-*

Stream, Vol. 19, No. 1 (January 1980), pp. 3-9.

24. Berard L. Marthaler, "Socialization as a Model of Catechetics," *Foundations of Religious Education,* ed. by Padraic O'Hare (Paulist Press, 1978), pp. 64-65.

25. Russell, *Human Liberation,* pp. 50-56.

26. Children's sermons designed by Shannon Clarkson, First Congregational Church of West Haven, Connecticut, 1979-1980.

27. Letty M. Russell, "Ministry for Social Change" (lecture at Yale Divinity School, 1979).

28. House Bible Study groups in the East Harlem Protestant Parish. Cf. Russell, *Christian Education in Mission,* pp. 107-113.

29. Groome, *Christian Religious Education,* pp. 109-115; cf. Marthaler, "Socialization as a Model of Catechetics," pp. 66-73.

30. Peter L. Berger, *The Sacred Canopy* (Doubleday & Co., 1967), pp. 3-28. Berger speaks of the three movements of socialization as externalization, objectification, and internalization.

31. Freire, *Pedagogy of the Oppressed,* p. 19. Cf. Peter Berger, "The False Consciousness of 'Consciousness Raising,' " *Mission Trends, No. 4: Liberation Theologies,* ed. by Gerald H. Anderson and Thomas F. Stransky (Paulist Press and Wm. B. Eerdmans Publishing Co., 1979), pp. 96-110.

32. Russell, *Human Liberation,* pp. 113-121. The idea of the dialectic of liberation was suggested to me by Rosemary Ruether's description of a "dialectic of oppression" in "Women's Liberation in Historical and Cultural Perspective," *Women's Liberation and the Church,* ed. by Sally Bentley Doely (Association Press, 1971), pp. 33-36.

33. Russell, *Partnership,* pp. 126-129.

34. Miller, *Toward a New Psychology of Women,* p. 125.

35. Dorothee Soelle, *Suffering,* tr. by Everett R. Kalin (Fortress Press, 1975), pp. 70-74.

36. Hodgson, *New Birth of Freedom,* pp. 2-42; Glenn R. Bucher (ed.), *Straight/White/Male* (Fortress Press, 1976); Russell, *Human Liberation,* p. 72.

37. Christy Ramage, Yale Divinity School, 1979. The contrast between *Performance* and *Partnership* was suggested

by Kathleen Corcoran, Yale Divinity School, 1980.

38. Irene W. Foulkes, "PRODIADIS, A New Way of Doing Theological Education in Latin America," *Ministerial Formation,* Vol. 5 (January 1979; World Council of Churches, Programme on Theological Education), pp. 12-15. Programa Diversificado a Distancia, Seminario Bíblico Latinamerico, Apartado 901, San José, Costa Rica. Cf. MAV, Master of Arts in Education for Human Values, San Francisco Theological Seminary, San Anselmo, California.

39. Brueggemann, *The Prophetic Imagination,* p. 14.

40. Harris, *Portrait of Ministry,* Ch. 7, "Diakonia: The Ministry of Troublemaking."

41. Brueggemann, *The Prophetic Imagination,* p. 13. Italics in the original.

42. Ibid, p. 12.

43. "Reflections and Problems of a Church Being Born Among the People" (Centro de Capacitación Social Ediciones, "CCS," Panama, July 1978). Translated and reproduced by Ecumenical Program for Interamerican Communication and Action (EPICA), 1470 Irving Street, N.W., Washington, D.C. 20010. Cf. Sergio Torres and John Eagelson (eds.), *The Challenge of Basic Christian Communities* (Orbis Books, 1981).

44. Faith Annette Sand with William Cook, "Winds of Change in Latin America," *The Other Side,* Vol. 16, No. 4 (April 1980), pp. 14-23.

45. José Marins, *Iglesia Local de Base* (Buenos Aires: Editorial Bonum, 1969), pp. 29-31. Cited by Mary J. Cuda, "Some Assumptions of Basic Christian Communities" (Unpublished paper, Yale Divinity School, April 30, 1979).

46. Sand and Cook, "Winds of Change in Latin America," pp. 16-17.

47. "The International Ecumenical Congress of Theology," February 20 to March 2, 1980, São Paulo, Brazil (The Ecumenical Association of Third World Theologians, 475 Riverside Drive, New York, NY 10115), p. 4. Cf. Marina Lessa, "Information About New Ministries and Small Base Communities in Brazil," *Women in Dialogue: Inter-American Meeting* (The Catholic Committee on Urban Ministry, 1112 Memorial Library, Notre Dame, Indiana, 1979).

48. Esther and Mortimer Arias, *The Cry of My People* (Friendship Press, 1980), p. 92. Cf. Wilson T. Boots, "Four Women Confront a Nation," *Christianity and Crisis,* Vol. 38, No. 7 (May 1, 1978).

49. Hoekendijk, *The Church Inside Out,* p. 188.

4. THEOLOGY AS ANTICIPATION

1. Informal conversation with the late Cyril Richardson, professor of church history, Union Theological Seminary, New York City, 1975.

2. Brueggemann, *The Prophetic Imagination,* pp. 32-37.

3. Von Rad, *Old Testament Theology,* Vol. II, pp. 210-212.

4. Phyllis Trible, *God and the Rhetoric of Sexuality* (Fortress Press, 1978), pp. 40-47.

5. Translation by Trible, ibid., p. 47.

6. William L. Holladay, "Jeremiah and Women's Liberation," *Andover Newton Quarterly,* Vol. 12, No. 4 (March 1972), pp. 213-233.

7. Trible, *God and the Rhetoric of Sexuality,* pp. 49-50; John Bright, *Jeremiah,* Vol. 21, *The Anchor Bible* (Doubleday & Co., 1965), p. 282. Bright says, "Quite possibly we have here a proverbial saying indicating something that is surprising and difficult to believe, the force of which escapes us."

8. W. L. Holladay, "New Covenant, The" IDBS, p. 623.

9. Wolfgang Roth and Rosemary Radford Ruether, *The Liberating Bond: Covenants—Biblical and Contemporary* (Friendship Press, 1978), pp. 17-19.

10. O. A. Piper, "Knowledge," IDB, Vol. III, p. 43.

11. Gerhard von Rad, *Old Testament Theology,* Vol. II, tr. D. M. G. Stalker (Harper & Row, 1966), p. 213.

12. Robert McAfee Brown, *Theology in a New Key: Responding to Liberation Themes* (Westminster Press, 1978), pp. 90-92; José Porfirio Miranda, *Marx and the Bible,* tr. by John Eagleson (Orbis Books, 1974), pp. 44-45.

13. Jorge Lara-Braud, "El Pueblo Unido Jamás Será Vencido," *Christianity and Crisis,* Vol. 40, No. 8 (May 12, 1980), pp. 114, 148-150. Cf. this entire issue which is on "Central America: A Season of Martyrs," and William J.

O'Malley, *The Voice of Blood: Five Christian Martyrs of Our Time* (Orbis Books, 1981).

14. Carol P. Christ and Judith Plaskow, *Womanspirit Rising: A Feminist Reader in Religion* (Harper & Row, 1979), Part IV, "Creating New Traditions," pp. 193-287.

15. Sr. Ann Patrick Ware, "Starting on a New Track" (Unpublished speech, National Council of Churches, Commission on Faith and Order, March 1980).

16. Rosemary Ruether, "A Religion for Women: Sources and Strategies," *Christianity and Crisis*, Vol. 39, No. 19 (Dec. 10, 1979), p. 309.

17. M. Douglas Meeks, "How to Speak of God in an Affluent Society," *The Witness*, Vol. 62, No. 10 (October 1979), p. 9.

18. Letty M. Russell, "Introduction: The Liberating Word," *The Liberating Word*, ed. by Letty M. Russell (Westminster Press, 1976), pp. 13-22.

19. Sharon H. Ringe, "Biblical Authority and Interpretation," *The Liberating Word*, ed. by Russell, p. 27.

20. *Daily Bible Readings: Inner City Parishes* (The East Harlem Protestant Parish, 2050 Second Avenue, New York, N.Y. 10029. Drawings by Joseph Papin, 1960-1968.

21. Sanders, "Hermeneutics," IDBS, p. 405.

22. Ibid., pp. 405-407.

23. P. Trible, "God, Nature of, in the OT, " IDBS, pp. 368-369; cf. Trible, *God and the Rhetoric of Sexuality*, pp. xv-xvii.

24. Russell, *Partnership*, pp. 49-53, 167-176.

25. Russell, *Human Liberation*, pp. 73-80.

26. Letty M. Russell, "Eschatological Hermeneutics" (Unpublished paper presented at the Liberation Theology Working Group, American Academy of Religion, March 1979). The art of anticipation is related to the development of the "hermeneutic of suspicion" by Segundo and other liberation theologians. Cf. Juan Luis Segundo, *The Liberation of Theology* (Orbis Books, 1976); Brown, *Theology in a New Key;* "Statement by Beatriz Melano Couch," *Theology in the Americas,* ed. by Sergio Torres and John Eagleson (Orbis Books, 1976); Dorothee Soelle, *Political Theology*, tr. by John R. Shelly (Fortress Press, 1974); Justo L. Gonzalez and

Catherine Gunsalus Gonzalez, *Liberation Preaching: The Pulpit and the Oppressed* (Abingdon Press, 1980), pp. 69-93.
27. Conversation with Walter Harrelson, Pacific School of Religion, July 1977.
28. Trible, *God and the Rhetoric of Sexuality,* Chs. 5 and 6.
29. Jon Sobrino, *Christology at the Crossroads: A Latin American Approach* (Orbis Books, 1978), p. 40, fn. 42. Sobrino is quoting Ignacio Ellacuria, "The *Verbum* of the Bible is not *Factum* already given, but *Faciendum* (something to be done)."
30. "The Effects of Women's Studies on Biblical Studies" (Unpublished papers at the Society for Biblical Literature, Dallas, 1980). This panel, chaired by Phyllis Trible, focused on the continuing task of feminist hermeneutic.
31. Leander E. Keck, *The Bible in the Pulpit: The Renewal of Biblical Preaching* (Abingdon Press, 1978); Walter Wink, *The Bible in Human Transformation: Toward a New Paradigm for Biblical Study* (Fortress Press, 1973).
32. Boys, *Biblical Interpretation in Religious Education;* Groome, *Christian Religious Education,* pp. 195-197.
33. Fiorenza, "Eschatology of the NT," IDBS, pp. 271-277.
34. Russell, *Human Liberation,* pp. 106-113. Richard P. McBrien lists five types of eschatology currently used in theology: (1) consistent, consequent, futurist, or thoroughgoing; (2) realized; (3) existentialist; (4) salvation-history; (5) proleptic. These are similar to the types of eschatology I list in *Partnership* (apocalyptic, teleological, axiological, adventological) except that McBrien divides the last category into salvation-history and proleptic eschatology. A community of anticipation would be one in which proleptic eschatology is the predominant emphasis, anticipating the *not yet, already* in the present (Richard P. McBrien, *Church: The Continuing Quest,* Newman Press, 1970, pp. 14-21; Russell, *Partnership,* pp. 168-170).
35. David Kelsey, "The Bible and Christian Ideology," *The Journal of the American Academy of Religion,* Vol. 48, No. 3 (1980), pp. 385-402.
36. Letty M. Russell, "Tradition as Mission: Study of a New Current in Theology and Its Implications for Theological

Education" (Unpublished doctoral dissertation, Union Theological Seminary, New York City, 1969), pp. 329-336.

37. Eleanore McGaffin, First Congregational Church of West Haven, Connecticut.

5. PEDAGOGY FOR OPPRESSORS

1. James Hood, "Reflections on Partnership" (Unpublished paper, Yale Divinity School, October 1980). Used by permission.

2. Freire, *Pedagogy of the Oppressed*, pp. 39-40.

3. Ibid., p. 42.

4. Russell, *Partnership*, pp. 126-127.

5. Krister Stendahl, "Liberation Is for the Oppressed," and "Freedom as an Excuse for Privilege" (Unpublished lectures, Augustana College, Sioux Falls, South Dakota, July 8-9, 1979).

6. Hodgson, *New Birth of Freedom*.

7. In the Hebrew text for Isa. 61:1, the phrase "bind up the brokenhearted" appears. It does not appear in Luke 4:18 (RSV), which follows the Greek version of Isaiah.

8. I. Howard Marshall, *The Gospel of Luke: A Commentary on the Greek Text* (Wm. B. Eerdmans Publishing Co., 1978), pp. 181-184.

9. John H. Yoder, *The Politics of Jesus* (Wm. B. Eerdmans Publishing Co., 1972), pp. 34-40.

10. Marshall, *The Gospel of Luke*, pp. 244-246.

11. *Alleluia: Hymnbook for Inner City Parishes,* ed. by The East Harlem Protestant Parish (Delaware, Ohio: Cooperative Recreation Service, 1962), "Parish Purpose," p. 12; "Rise, Shine for Thy Light Is A-Commin'," Negro Spiritual, p. 86.

12. Yoder, *The Politics of Jesus*, p. 36.

13. Ibid., p. 38; cf. Russell, *Partnership*, pp. 152-155.

14. Birch and Rasmussen, *The Predicament of the Prosperous,* p. 88. Sharon Ringe, "The Jubilee Proclamation in the Ministry and Teaching of Jesus: A Tradition Critical Study in the Synoptic Gospels and Acts" (Unpublished dissertation, Union Theological Seminary, New York City, 1980), "Conclusion."

15. Marshall, *The Gospel of Luke*, p. 184.

16. Brueggemann, *The Prophetic Imagination*, p. 83;

Stendahl, *Paul Among Jews and Gentiles*, pp. 100-102.

17. Jürgen Moltmann with M. Douglas Meeks, "The Liberation of Oppressors," *Christianity and Crisis*, Vol. 38, No. 20 (Dec. 25, 1978), p. 317.

18. Johannes Christiaan Hoekendijk, "Mission—A Celebration of Freedom," *Union Seminary Quarterly Review*, Vol. 21, No. 2, Part I (January 1966), pp. 140-141. Cf. Brueggemann, *The Prophetic Imagination*, p. 17.

19. Marshall, *The Gospel of Luke*, pp. 184-190.

20. S. MacLean Gilmour, "The Gospel According to Luke," *The Interpreter's Bible*, ed. by George Arthur Buttrick (Abingdon Press, 1952), Vol. VIII, p. 95.

21. Letty M. Russell, "God's Call and the Future of the Church," 1976 Institute of Theology, Princeton Theological Seminary.

22. Dorothee Soelle, "Exodus," *Revolutionary Patience*, tr. by Rita and Robert Kimber (Orbis Books, 1977); cf. "Resistance: Toward a First World Theology," *Christianity and Crisis*, Vol. 39, No. 12 (July 23, 1979), pp. 178-182.

23. Stendahl, "Judgement and Mercy," *Paul Among Jews and Gentiles*, pp. 103-106.

24. Birch and Rasmussen, *The Predicament of the Prosperous;* Stendahl, *Paul Among Jews and Gentiles*, p. 105.

25. Marie Augusta Neal, *A Socio-Theology of Letting Go: The Role of a First World Church Facing Third World Peoples* (Paulist Press, 1977), p. 106.

26. The game was developed by Carol Adams and Jim Hood, Yale Divinity School, 1980.

27. Edward R. Norman, "A Politicized Christ," *Christianity and Crisis*, Vol. 39, No. 2 (Feb. 19, 1979), pp. 18-25. Cf. responses to Norman by Dorothee Soelle, Peter Berger, Roger Shinn, Arthur Cochrane, John Fry in *Christianity and Crisis*, Vol. 39, No. 4 (March 19, 1979), and Vol. 39, No. 6 (April 16, 1979).

28. *Third World* refers to people living outside North America and Western Europe (*First World*) and of the Communist bloc countries in Eastern Europe (*Second World*), and includes their descendants as well as indigenous populations living in racial oppression in any country. (Russell, *Human Liberation*, pp. 20-21.) In speaking of

themselves, Third World persons often prefer to use the term *Two-Thirds World* as an indication of their majority in population and as a rejection of the white, Western world as "first." Women sometimes speak of themselves as *Fourth World*, an oppressed majority living in all the other worlds.

29. Daniel L. Migliore, *Called to Freedom: Liberation Theology and the Future of Christian Doctrine* (Westminster Press, 1980); all the other books have already been cited above. For an attempt to criticize liberation theologies, not in their own framework, but in the framework of process theology, see Shubert M. Ogden, *Faith and Freedom: Toward a Theology of Liberation* (Abingdon Press, 1979).

30. Torres and Eagleson, *Theology in the Americas;* "Radical Christians: What Has Happened to Them? What Lies Ahead?" *JSAC Grapevine*, Vol. 11, No. 10 (May 1980); *Is Liberation Theology for North America?* (Theology in the Americas, 475 Riverside Drive, New York, N.Y. 10115, 1978).

31. Soelle, *Political Theology;* "Resistance Toward a First World Theology"; Neal, *A Socio-Theology of Letting Go;* "Theology of Relinquishment: Prophetic Role of the Church," *Is Liberation Theology for North America?* pp. 123-133.

32. Moltmann with M. Douglas Meeks, "The Liberation of Oppressors," p. 310. Cf. Jürgen Moltmann, "On Latin American Liberation Theology: An Open Letter to José Miguez-Bonino," *Christianity and Crisis,* Vol. 36, No. 5 (March 29, 1976), pp. 57-62, and "Hope in the Struggle of the People," *Christianity and Crisis,* Vol. 37, No. 4 (March 21, 1977), pp. 49-54; M. Douglas Meeks, "The Holy Spirit and Human Needs: Toward a Trinitarian View of Economics," *Christianity and Crisis,* Vol. 40, No. 18 (Nov. 10, 1980), pp. 307-316.

33. Moltmann with M. Douglas Meeks, "The Liberation of Oppressors," p. 311.

34. Ibid., p. 313.

35. Ibid., p. 316.

36. Charles Brown, Yale Divinity School, April, 1980. Unpublished book abstract (draft); tentative title: "The Moral Reality of Power." Cf. Russell, *Partnership*, pp. 67-70.

37. Betty Lehan Harragan, *Games Mother Never Taught You: Corporate Gamesmanship for Women* (Warner Books, 1977).

38. Ibid., pp. 96-116.

39. Ibid., pp. 382-383.

40. Miller, *Toward a New Psychology of Women,* pp. 115-124. Cf. The Cornwall Collective, *Your Daughters Shall Prophesy: Feminist Alternatives in Theological Education* (Pilgrim Press, 1980), pp. 70-76.

41. Ibid., p. 124.

42. This idea of the advantage of women being status inconsistent was suggested by Dorothee Soelle at the AAR/SBL Working Group on Liberation Theology, New York City, November 1979.

43. Bucher, *Straight/White/Male,* pp. vii-viii.

44. Greenleaf, *Servant Leadership,* pp. 7-48.

45. Groome, *Christian Religious Education,* pp. 207-232.

46. Neil Postman and Charles Weingartner, *Teaching as a Subversive Activity* (Delacorte Press, 1969). Cf. Paulo Freire, *Education for Critical Consciousness,* tr. Myra Ramos (Seabury Press, 1973).

47. T. Richard Snyder, "Theological Education and Caesar's Household," *The Witness,* Vol. 62, No. 10 (October 1979), pp. 4-7; Gonzalez and Gonzalez, *Liberation Preaching.*

48. Jürgen Moltmann, *Theology of Hope,* tr. by James W. Leitch (Harper & Row, 1967), p. 17.

49. *The City—God's Gift to the Church* (Board of National Missions, The United Presbyterian Church in the U.S.A., 475 Riverside Drive, New York, N.Y. 10115, 1964).

50. Marianne Stern, First Congregational Church of West Haven, Connecticut, 1979.

51. Bucher, *Straight/White/Male,* pp. 23-27. Cf. Jane Sullivan, "Internship at YDS" (Unpublished paper, Yale Divinity School, 1981).

52. Virginia R. Mollenkott, *Speech, Silence, Action!* (Abingdon Press, 1980), Ch. 4.

53. In our class on Education for Partnership, Jim Hood and Sara Beth Terrell said that sharing the questions together was an important aspect of becoming partners in marriage (Yale Divinity School, 1980). Cf. Thomas S. Kuhn, The

Structure of Scientific Revolutions, 2d ed. (University of Chicago Press, 1970), pp. 5-6; Lewis Thomas, *The Medusa and the Snail* (Bantam Books, 1980), pp. 29-32.

54. Russell, *Partnership*, pp. 140-141. Cf. Rainer Maria Rilke, *Letters to a Young Poet*, rev. ed., tr. by M. D. Herter Norton (W. W. Norton & Co., 1954), p. 35.

55. A free paraphrase by the author in consultation with Hans Hoekendijk. Cf. Hoekendijk, "Bible Study on Romans 8:13-27," *Concept* (Geneva: World Council of Churches, DSME/M69:25), pp. 20-25.

6. SPIRITUALITY OF LIBERATION

1. Cone, *God of the Oppressed*, pp. 17-23.

2. "The International Ecumenical Congress of Theology," São Paulo, Brazil, 1980, pp. 8-9. Cf. Migliore, *Called to Freedom*, pp. 81-99. Gustavo Gutiérrez, *A Theology of Liberation*, tr. and ed. by Caridad Inda and John Eagleson (Orbis Books, 1973), pp. 203-204.

3. Clare Benedicks Fisher et al. (eds.), *Women in a Strange Land* (Fortress Press, 1975); Rosemary Ruether and Eleanor McLaughlin (eds.), *Women of Spirit: Female Leadership in the Jewish and Christian Traditions* (Simon & Schuster, 1979).

4. From an informal talk by Professor Oo Chung Lee, in political exile in the U.S.A., at a meeting of the Ad Hoc Group of Racism, Sexism and Classism, December 1980, in New York City. Cf. Harold Hakwon Sunno and Dong Soo Kim (eds.), *Korean Women: A Struggle for Humanization* (The Korean Christian Scholars, Publication #3, Spring 1978).

5. Vincent Taylor, *The Gospel According to St. Mark* (London: Macmillan & Co., 1963), p. 277.

6. Marshall, *The Gospel of Luke*, pp. 338-339.

7. Geiko Müller-Fahrenholz, *Partners in Life: Handicapped and the Church* (World Council of Churches, Faith and Order Paper No. 89, 1979).

8. Marshall, *The Gospel of Luke*, p. 338.

9. Core Group at Yale–New Haven Hospital, October 1978.

10. C. E. B. Cranfield, *The Gospel According to Saint Mark* (Cambridge University Press, 1959), pp. 179-180.

11. Jürgen Moltmann, "Hope in the Struggle of the People," *Christianity and Crisis*, Vol. 37, No. 4 (March 21, 1977), p. 54.

12. "New Math Overthrown?" *Mother Jones*, Vol. 5, No. 6 (July 1980), p. 10.

13. Hoekendijk, *Horizons of Hope,* p. 45.

14. Migliore, *Called to Freedom,* p. 93; Michael Collins Reilly, *Spirituality for Mission* (Orbis Books, 1978), pp. 22-45.

15. Johannes B. Metz, *Theology of the World,* tr. by William Glen-Doepal (Herder & Herder, 1969), pp. 102-104. Elizabeth Ingersoll, "In Search of a Usable Past" (Unpublished paper on the Spirituality of Catherine of Sienna, Yale Divinity School, 1980).

16. Camilo Torres, *Revolutionary Writings* (Herder & Herder, 1969), p. 168. Quoted in *The Radical Bible*, comp. by John Eagleson and Philip Scharper (Orbis Books, 1972), p. 76.

17. Soelle, *Suffering*, p. 17. The Dimensions of Suffering are from Simone Weil, "The Love of God and Affliction," *Waiting for God* (G. P. Putnam's Sons, 1951), p. 177.

18. Soelle, *Suffering,* p. 134. Cf. Tine Kamphuis, "Perspectives on Solidarity" (Unpublished dissertation, Utrecht, Aug. 11, 1980), pp. 72-84.

19. The idea that the danger of liberation theologies is "cheap hope," just as the danger of Lutheran theologies is "cheap grace" was pointed out by Eric Jorstad, "The Liberation of the *Augsburg Confession: Sola Gratia* as Social Transformation" (Unpublished paper, Yale Divinity School, December 1979). Cf. Dietrich Bonhoeffer, *The Cost of Discipleship* (London: SCM Press, 1959), p. 35.

20. Soelle, *Suffering,* pp. 70-74; cf. also Elisabeth Kübler-Ross, *On Death and Dying* (Macmillan Co., 1969).

21. Soelle, *Suffering,* p. 74.

22. Lawton W. Posey, "Deafness: Physical and Spiritual," *The Christian Century*, Vol. 97, No. 9 (March 12, 1980), pp. 278-279.

23. Edward Dobihal, "Hospice: Systemic Change by

Infection" (Unpublished speech at Yale Divinity School, November 9, 1979). Cf. "Facts About the Connecticut Hospice, Inc." (765 Prospect Street, New Haven, Conn. 06511).

24. Betty Rollin, "The Best Years of My Life," *The New York Times Magazine,* April 6, 1980, pp. 36-37.

25. Bruce Kenrick, *Come out the Wilderness: The Story of East Harlem Protestant Parish* (Harper & Row, 1962).

26. Ibid., title page. Cf. *Alleluia,* ed. by the East Harlem Protestant Parish, p. 67.

27. Harvey Perkins, Harry Daniel, and Asal Simandjuntak, "Let My People Go," *Mission Trends No. 3: Third World Theologies,* ed. by Gerald H. Anderson and Thomas F. Stransky (Paulist Press and Wm. B. Eerdmans Publishing Co., 1976), p. 194.

28. Letty M. Russell, "Called to Account," *The Ecumenical Review,* Vol. 30, No. 4 (October 1978), pp. 369-375. The problem of combining the different perspectives was underlined for me at the National Council of Churches Commission on Faith and Order meeting on "Spirituality for Ecumenism," March 1980, Marriottsville, Maryland.

29. Theressa Hoover, "Black Women and the Churches: Triple Jeopardy," *Black Theology: A Documentary History, 1966-1979,* ed. by Gayraud S. Wilmore and James H. Cone (Orbis Books, 1979), pp. 377-388.

30. The Cornwall Collective, *Your Daughters Shall Prophesy,* Preface.

31. Ibid., pp. 96-107.

32. Beverly W. Harrison and W. Robert Martin, Jr., "Is Theological Education Good for Any Woman's Health?" *Newsletter* (Center for Women and Religion, Graduate Theological Union, Berkeley, California), Spring 1978. Cf. James H. Cone, "New Roles in Ministry: A Theological Appraisal," Wilmore and Cone, *Black Theology,* p. 392.

33. The idea that racism, sexism, and classism are not problems to be solved but conditions of collective sin was suggested by Freda Gardiner, Princeton Theological Seminary, April 1980.

34. Steven Mackie, "Caught in a Webb . . . ?" *RISK,* Vol. 10, No. 3 (1974), pp. 36-43; Letty M. Russell, "Human

Liberation in a Feminine Perspective," *Study Encounter*, Vol. 7, No. 1 (1972).

35. This phrase was suggested by Margaret Farley in a sermon at Yale Divinity School, February 1980. It is from a personal conversation between Ursala Niebuhr and Christopher Mooney. (Christopher F. Mooney, *Man Without Tears* p. 69; Harper & Row, 1975.)

36. Judith O'Neill, Interview on Ministry for Social Change at University of Massachusetts (Yale Divinity School, 1980).

37. Roy DeLamotte, "Can Blacks Escape the Mainstream?" *The Christian Century,* Vol. 97, No. 9 (March 12, 1980), pp. 276-277; cf. "Moving Toward Partnership," *Racism/Sexism: A Resource Packet for Leaders* (United Church Board for Homeland Ministries, 1979), Section VII.

38. Peggy Billings, "Working for Social Justice in the Bureaucracy" (Speech delivered at the RSAC Advance, June 1980).

39. Jane Middletown in a private conversation, September 1979.

40. Robert McAfee Brown, "The Spirit's Eighth Gift," *Christianity and Crisis,* Vol. 40, No. 1 (Feb. 4, 1980), p. 8.

41. A free paraphrase by the author in partnership with Hans Hoekendijk.